HORIZON

NOVEMBER, 1959 • VOLUME II, NUMBER 2

HORIZON
A Magazine of the Arts

NOVEMBER, 1959 · VOLUME II, NUMBER 2

PUBLISHER
James Parton

EDITOR
Joseph J. Thorndike, Jr.

MANAGING EDITOR
William Harlan Hale

ASSOCIATE EDITORS
Ralph Backlund
Robert Emmett Ginna

ASSISTANT EDITORS
Ada Pesin
Jane Wilson

EDITORIAL ASSISTANTS
Shirley Abbott, Caroline Backlund,
Martha Thomson

COPY EDITOR
Patricia M. Graves
Assistants: Rebecca R. Barocas
Mary Ann Pfeiffer

ART DIRECTOR
Irwin Glusker
Assistant: Emma Landau

ADVISORY BOARD
Gilbert Highet, *Chairman*
Frederick Burkhardt   Oliver Jensen
Marshall B. Davidson   Jotham Johnson
Richard M. Ketchum

EUROPEAN CONSULTING EDITOR
J. H. Plumb
Christ's College, Cambridge

EUROPEAN BUREAU
Gertrudis Feliu, *Chief*
28 Quai du Louvre, Paris

CIRCULATION DIRECTOR
Richard V. Benson

HORIZON is published every two months by American Horizon, Inc., a subsidiary of American Heritage Publishing Co., Inc., 551 Fifth Avenue, New York 17, N. Y.
Single Copies: $3.95
Annual Subscriptions: $18.00 in the U.S. & Can.
$19.00 elsewhere

Second-Class postage paid at New York, N.Y.

COVER: "And for the drink-offering thou shalt present the third part of a hin of wine, of a sweet savour unto the Lord." In an action of final libation resembling that prescribed for the Hebrews in Numbers 15:7, Nebamun, superintendent of sculptors in Egypt, pours wine on the sacrificial pile of animals and meal. As if to insure his safe passage to the other world, the ritual is executed to perfection under the watchful eye of Nebamun's mother, the house-mistress, Thepu. This Egyptian wall painting of the Nineteenth Dynasty is from the Tomb of the Two Sculptors near Thebes. An article on current progress in the field of Biblical archaeology begins on page 4.

FRONTISPIECE: With feathered headdresses and scarves flying, horsemen of the Medici Court execute a graceful equestrian ballet, probably before the visiting Archduke Ferdinand of Tyrol, his wife Anna, and the German bishop Sigismund in 1652. This drawing was one of many sketched by the noted Florentine engraver and court artist, Stefano della Bella, who fashioned the rhythmic patterns especially for the Medici cavalry. This corps brought the *Balletto a Cavallo* to a high point of spectacle emulated throughout Europe. The water color is in the collection of Francis Stonor, London.

THE BIBLE
AS DIVINING ROD

*By following clues in the Scriptures, archaeologists
are lighting up the ancient history of the Holy Land*

By NELSON GLUECK

Above the barren range of Jebel Ideid in the Negev, Nelson Glueck (center) and his associates view this ancient trade route

Shortly before the turn of the century a native boy stumbled while wading through a tunnel leading underground from a pool of water south of the Old City of Jerusalem—and made an exceedingly important archaeological discovery. As he got to his feet, the lad noticed on the wall of the tunnel what appeared to be ancient letters cut into the rock. His employer, a German architect named Conrad Schick, identified the writing as six lines of ancient Hebrew, incised on a smoothed portion of the wall in a space a little larger than the page of a modern newspaper. The inscription was located above the offset in the tunnel, where two working parties who were quarrying from opposite ends, long centuries ago, met each other at a point almost equidistant from the tunnel openings—a remarkably early example of good engineering.

The first part of the inscription was missing, but the remainder was clear enough to be read easily. Its translation, in part, is as follows:

When the tunnel was driven through . . . and while there were still three cubits to be cut through, there was heard the voice of a man calling to his fellow, for there was an overlap in the rock on the right and on the left. And when the tunnel was driven through, the quarrymen hewed the rock, each man toward his fellow, axe against axe; and the water flowed from the spring toward the reservoir for 1,200 cubits, and the height of the rock above the heads of the quarrymen was 100 cubits.

While neither names nor dates are mentioned in the inscription on the wall, we know from the Bible just about when and under whose direction the tunnel was cut. This ancient and difficult underground public works project was carried out more than twenty-seven hundred years ago, near the end of the eighth century B.C. The pertinent passages in Sacred Writ, one in II Kings 20:20 and another in II Chronicles 32:30, fill in the story. The first passage reads:

Now the rest of the acts of Hezekiah, and all his might, and how he made the pool and the tunnel and brought water into the city, *are* they not written in the Book of Chronicles of the Kings of Judah?

And the second passage reads:

This same Hezekiah also stopped the upper spring of the waters of Gihon, and brought them straight down on the west side of the city of David.

Fearing what actually occurred, namely that the Assyrian king, Sennacherib, would attack the city of Jerusalem, Hezekiah had a tunnel dug, some 1,750 feet long, leading the spring of Gihon into the Pool of Siloam within the city walls, and assured the city a supply of water even during a time of siege.

Some years ago, I waded through this tunnel of Siloam, thinking to examine the inscription. I had completely forgotten that about ten years after it had been discovered, some vandals had cut it out and carted it away. Fortunately, the pieces were confiscated by the Turkish authorities and brought to Istanbul, where I finally viewed them in their restored form in the museum there. The Biblical statements and this rock-hewn memorial tablet form a classic example of how historical memories and records in scriptural accounts are confirmed or supplemented or clarified by archaeological finds.

The Bible, of course, is essentially a theological document devoted to the exposition of the nature and moral imperatives of God. It is only secondarily a book of history and geography. Selected historical materials were incorporated into the Biblical text for the sole purpose of illustrating and underlining the kind of religious teaching of the Biblical books passionately believed to be divinely ordained.

Historians, nevertheless, and archaeologists in particular, have learned to rely upon the amazing accuracy of historical memory in the Bible. The most fleeting references to persons and places and events contained in the accounts of the Exodus, for instance, or the biographies of such Biblical heroes as Abraham and Moses and David, can lead, if properly considered and pursued, to immensely important historical discoveries. The archaeologists' efforts are not directed at "proving" the correctness of the Bible, which is neither necessary nor possible, any more than belief in God can be scientifically demonstrated. It is quite the other way around. The historical clues in the Bible can lead the archaeologist to a knowledge of the civilizations of the ancient world in which the Bible developed and with whose religious concepts and practices the Bible so radically differed. It can be regarded in effect as an almost infallible divining rod, revealing to the expert the whereabouts and characteristics of lost cities and civilizations.

The Bible recounts in Genesis 14 a savage incursion of the Kings of the East in the time of Abraham. In recent years William F. Albright and I have retraced the route of march from Syria to Sinai and discovered a whole series of villages which were occupied in the twenty-first to nineteenth centuries B.C. and were completely destroyed at the end of that period. The archaeological discoveries correspond perfectly to the narrative in Genesis. When we reflect on the means by which the Biblical account has reached us, its accuracy is indeed astounding. For this upheaval in what archaeologists call the Middle Bronze Age I, occurred at least a thousand years before the earliest written Biblical records. Thus, for many centuries, by word of mouth from father to son and by recitals of wandering minstrels, the story of the catastrophic conflict was transmitted from generation to generation until it achieved immortality in the Biblical scrolls. Even the names of the dramatis personae and the places they appeared in were repeated year after year in the form of a sacred and unchanging liturgical ritual.

Recent years have seen a great and immensely fruitful burst of archaeological activity in the Holy Land. The discovery of the Dead Sea Scrolls was only the most dramatic of many discoveries which throw light on the beginnings of Judaism, Christianity, and Islam. It is worth emphasizing that in all this work no archaeological discovery has ever controverted a single, properly understood Biblical statement.

The relationship of even isolated historical allusions in the Bible to archaeological discoveries in Palestine has recently been emphasized anew by excavations at Gibeon conducted under the direction of James B. Pritchard, Professor of Near Eastern History at the Church Divinity School of the Pacific in Berkeley, California. There is reference in II Samuel to "the pool of Gibeon," by the side of which a bloody gladiatorial contest took place between adherents of Joab and Abner, who were mortal enemies. These two were commanding generals, respectively, of the army of David, who had just been crowned king of Judah, and of the army of Saul's pathetic son, Ish-bosheth. The latter, after his father and his brothers had met their deaths in the disastrous battle of Gilboa between the Philistines and the Israelites, remained the sole obstacle in the path of David's becoming king also of Israel and the head of what subsequently developed under him into the United Kingdom of Judah and Israel. The pertinent passages read as follows:

And Abner . . . went out from Mahanaim to Gibeon. And Joab . . . and the servants of David went out; and they met together by the pool of Gibeon and took their positions, the one group on the one side of the pool and the other group on the other side of the pool. And Abner said to Joab: "Let the young men, I pray thee, arise and let them play before us." And Joab said, "Let them arise." Which they did, and passed over by number: twelve for . . . Ish-bosheth the son of Saul and twelve of the servants of

6

PHOTOGRAPHS BY NELSON GLUECK

Reading from the Bible in the desert above the shores of the Red Sea, Nelson Glueck briefs his archaeological team during their search for historical sites. An area of King Solomon's copper mines (lower left) has been identified at Timnah in the Wadi Araba, and the slanting rock walls of Ain Yerka (lower right) guard a precious spring used by desert wanderers and their flocks.

THE POOL OF GIBEON

At modern el-Jib in Jordan, corresponding to the ancient city of Gibeon, an American expedition unearthed the famous Biblical pool. In case of siege, the entrance was shut off and access to the waters gained through a tunnel (below).

David. And they caught every one his opposite number by the head and thrust his sword into his opponent's side, with the result that they all fell down together; wherefore that place was called The Field of Sharp Knives, which is in Gibeon. And the battle was very sore that day; and Abner and the men of Israel were beaten before the servants of David (II Samuel 2:12–17).

We owe the survival of this account to the Biblical writers' preoccupation with David and his role in Israelitic history. As the gifted leader of his people, the progenitor of its noblest strain, who had been brought low and was penitent, David was one of the great heroes of the Biblical narrative. No detail was too small to be included in his spiritual biography. David and his household were become God's chosen instrument and the Bible followed his progress through sin and suffering, through conquest and cupidity, through arrogance and humility, all his livelong days (II Samuel 7:12–15).

If it seems beyond belief that the account of the struggle at Gibeon should have survived in such detail for generations before it was written down, I can only say that I have witnessed the same transmission of history among the modern Bedouins. I have sat hundreds of times in Arab tents and heard raconteurs recite, with the rhythm of poetry and the minute detail of a police blotter, events of their own time and their ancestors'. Frequently, in response to my questioning, I would hear the same story told over and over again in widely removed encampments with hardly a hairsbreadth of difference in the description of a fight, a feast, a birth, or a death.

The Pool of Gibeon became, quite reasonably, a prize of the archaeologist's seeking. Its location had escaped the memories of man for many centuries, and the search itself was an ancient one. An early Palestinian historian, Eusebius, Bishop of Caesarea in the fourth century A.D., had suggested in his famous *Onomasticon* that Biblical Gibeon was four miles west of Bethel, at the modern Arabic village of el-Bireh. One argues reluctantly with the Bishop of Caesarea, who lived fifteen hundred years nearer to the Biblical period, but the great American scholar Edward Robinson did so, and suggested that a likelier site was the modern village of el-Jib, north of Jerusalem.

A couple of years ago, Pritchard and his colleagues determined to test the correctness of this thesis by conducting excavations on the site of the village of el-Jib—and their soundings struck gold, the gold of history. On the handle of wine jars they came upon that most unusual of all archaeological finds —the actual name of the ancient town. The jars had been fashioned for the export of the locally produced Gibeon wine.

To cap the climax, the modern archaeologists discovered and reopened the "Pool of Gibeon." It was 36 feet in diameter at the top and 35 feet deep, with a spiral staircase leading downward around the inside face of the pool. And all of it had been carved out of the solid rock! When they got to the bottom of the staircase, the excavators found and cleared out a tunnel which curved downward for 49 feet more until it reached a chamber where a pool of water collects. That point is 84 feet below the top of the hill on which ancient Gibeon once stood.

In my own work Biblical clues have been equally fruitful. Like many others, I had long been puzzled by the vague description in the Bible of the Promised Land as "a land whose stones are iron and out of whose hills you can dig copper" (Deuteronomy 8:9). No copper or iron had ever been discovered in the Holy Land. Was the Biblical statement correct, or was it a figment of the imagination? Believing as I do in the historical memory of the Bible, I began to assemble all the Biblical passages which might cast some light upon the location of copper and iron deposits. There was a single reference to a "Valley of Smiths" (I Chronicles 4:14), and another to a "City of Copper" (I Chronicles 4:12), but no one had the foggiest notion where they were located or indeed if they had ever really existed. Nevertheless, as I studied all the Biblical references in relation to one another, the obscurity which veiled them seemed to become less dense and the possibility of discovering ancient mines in a particular region of the Holy Land seemed to become more real. And finally, a chain of clues was formed, which pointed the way to their discovery. Here is how the separate links appeared:

(a) The reference to "smiths" called to mind a descendant of Eve's son, Cain, whose name was Tubal-cain. According to the Bible, he was the first smith in the annals of human history, renowned as "the manufacturer of all kinds of copper and iron instruments" (Genesis 4:22). Indeed, the last part of his name, which in English is spelled "Cain" and could equally and perhaps more correctly be spelled "Ken," indicated that he was a smith by profession.

(b) "Ken" is also a form of the Biblical Hebrew word for a copper spear; the Kenites were a tribe of wandering smiths, who made spears and other metal implements, and whose territory was eastern Sinai, the Negev, and the Wadi Araba.

(c) It will be recalled that during the period of the Exodus through Sinai and the Negev, Moses had taken a wife from the Kenites (Judges 1:16), and that the Israelites afterward maintained the closest relationship with them (I Samuel 15:6).

(d) It was probably the Kenites and the related Kenizzites (Genesis 15:19) who introduced the Israelites to the arts of mining and metallurgy.

(e) It is reasonable furthermore to assume that it was from his in-laws, the Kenites, that Moses learned to make a copper serpent, which was used, so the Bible tells us, to heal those bitten by fiery serpents sent by the Lord to punish them for complaining against their hard lot during their Exodus journey (Numbers 21:5-9).

(f) The scene of this incident, to judge from the account in Numbers 21, is laid in the rift of the Wadi Araba, which extends from the south end of the Dead Sea to the north end of the Gulf of Aqaba.

(g) It should be noted in this connection, that one of the stations of the Exodus was Punon in the Araba rift, as mentioned in specific geographical context in Numbers 33:42.

HAZOR, CITY OF KINGS

Yigael Yadin, Israeli general and archaeologist, stands in an excavated trench on the site of the Canaanite city of Hazor in Galilee. Below, second from left, he supervises the digging near the walls built by a royal architect of King Solomon.

(h) If the assumption were correct that the copper serpent of Moses was made by him in the Araba part of the Exodus, then the likelihood existed that it was in the Araba, and with the assistance of the Kenites, that he obtained the copper he needed for the purpose.

(i) This suggested that the City of Copper of I Chronicles 4:12 might well be looked for in the Araba and that the Valley of Smiths of I Chronicles 4:14 might well be identified with the Valley of the Araba—a possibility which is heightened by the fact that there seems to be the memory in I Chronicles 4:13–15 of an association of the Kenizzites with the Valley of the Smiths.

(j) And lastly, if these various links of the chain of clues held together, then it was clear that the description in Deuteronomy 8:9 of a "land whose stones are iron and out of whose hills you can dig copper" could well apply to the Wadi Araba.

With all of these Biblical clues seeming to point in one direction, we decided to explore archaeologically the entire length and width of the Wadi Araba. We probably would have undertaken its exploration anyway in the course of tracing the Exodus, but the possibility of finding in the Araba the Biblical City of Copper and the Valley of Smiths and the deposits of iron and copper referred to in Deuteronomy added incentive to our undertaking.

As we rode day after day on camel-back through the Wadi Araba, our Arab companions kept telling us about a place called Khirbet Nahas, which means "Copper Ruin." To my repeated questions about the significance of the name, they could only answer that the place had always been called that. One day, after weary weeks of exploration, we approached Khirbet Nahas. In the distance we could make out heaps of black stones as well as a great stone wall and numerous small structures which looked like stone houses but were obviously too small to accommodate human beings. Dismounting and tying the legs of our camels together so that they could not run away, we soon realized that this was indeed the Biblical "City of Copper." The heaps of black stones were piles of slag of copper which had been mined in the vicinity and given a preliminary roasting in small stone ovens which looked like miniature houses; the remnants of the great stone wall enclosed an area where the slaves who worked the mines and the roasting ovens were kept when the day's work was over. Strewn about on the ground were fragments of pottery which enabled us to date this mining site to the time of King Solomon and his successors.

Not far away, we found iron deposits also. The reference in Deuteronomy was literally true, as were the references to a City of Copper and to a Valley of the Smiths, for that is what the Wadi Araba was. Khirbet Nahas was the first of a long series of similar sites which we found on both sides of the Araba rift as far south as the Gulf of Aqaba. The Bible had correctly recorded the existence of mineral deposits in the Promised Land. Indeed, the knowledge of their existence must have been so generally known and so widely spread, that the merest reference to them seemed to suffice in the minds of the Biblical editors. Extremely careful attention to the few Biblical verses dealing with copper and iron and smiths and objects made of copper and of people and places associated with them had led us to the discovery of what we have called King Solomon's Copper Mines.

Study of similar evidence led to the rediscovery of Solomon's long-lost port city of Ezion-geber on the north shore of the Gulf of Aqaba, which is the eastern arm of the Red Sea. Our clue was the Biblical reference to Solomon's port as lying "beside Eloth, on the shore of the Red Sea, in the land of Edom" (I Kings 9:26). Earlier archaeologists, misled by their theory that the shore of the Red Sea had retreated southward in the course of three thousand years, had looked for the site far up the rift of the Wadi Araba. But our discovery of a copper smelting site directly above the northwest shore of the gulf led us to conclude that the site of the port must be close to the present shore. There remained little for us to do except to search the north shore of the Gulf of Aqaba for the remains of an ancient site, which might correspond in time of occupation to that of Solomon's port city. It was not hard to find, and consisted of a small artificial city-hill, called Tell el-Khalifa, situated in the center of the north shore, only a few hundred yards removed from the waters of the gulf. To the German explorer Fritz Frank, however, goes the accolade of discovery. Several weeks before we arrived at Tell el-Khalifa, he had come across it and correctly suggested its identification with Ezion-geber, although we did not know about it at the time.

When we excavated Tell el-Khalifa, we discovered the largest copper smelter ever found in antiquity. Solomon was not only a very wise ruler and a very successful merchant and shipping magnate, as is known from Biblical passages, but was also, to judge from the copper mines in the Wadi Araba and the shipping and industrial center of Ezion-geber, a copper king of the ancient world. We are convinced that much of his power and the rise of the kingdom of Israel under his rule can be attributed to his masterful exploitation of mineral resources and to his exporting copper ingots and finished copper objects to Arabia and India and Africa in return for their precious products.

In another instance, the description in the Bible of the ancient city of Hazor, which was the capital of northern Canaan in the time of Joshua, helped archaeologists identify it with the great mound of Tell el-Qedah in eastern Galilee. Joshua conquered it and burned it with fire (Joshua 11: 10-11). Its importance was not truly restored until Solomon rebuilt and refortified it, together with Megiddo and Gezer, making them three of the major strongholds of his kingdom (I Kings 9:15).

Extensive excavations are being carried out there under the direction of that brilliant soldier-scholar, Yigael Yadin, former chief-of-staff of the Israeli Defense Forces. General

TEXT CONTINUED ON PAGE 118

ARCHAEOLOGY ILLUSTRATES THE BIBLE

The discoveries of modern archaeology have brought vividly to life many Biblical passages. In a series of volumes entitled *Views of the Biblical World,* the International Publishing Company in Israel has brought together many of the significant paintings and artifacts which have come to light in the lands of the Fertile Crescent, from Mesopotamia to Egypt. (Because the Israelites forbade all images, few are from the Holy Land itself.) This major work of scholarship has drawn on the resources of scholars and museums in many countries. The illustrations on this and the following eight pages are taken from the first published volume: *The Law.*

Now the serpent was more subtle than any beast of the field which the Lord God had made. And he tempted the woman to eat of the forbidden fruit. . . . In his wrath, the Lord condemned the serpent: Because thou hast done this, cursed art thou . . . among all beasts of the field; upon thy belly shalt thou go, and dust shalt thou eat all the days of thy life.
(GEN. 3:1, 14)

In ancient Talmudic legend, the snake was a symbol of evil that walked upright and had a brain superior to that of all other animals. It was envy of man that caused the snake to plot his downfall in the Garden of Eden, thereupon invoking the punishment, "upon thy belly shalt thou go." This legendary snake of glazed brick, with the forelegs of a lion and the hind legs of an eagle, was found on the Gate of Ishtar in Babylon and dates from the sixth century B.C. It is now in the collection of the Detroit Arts Institute.

This is the book of the generations of Adam. In the day that God created man, in the likeness of God made He him; male and female created He them, and blessed them, and called their name Adam. . . . And Adam . . . begot a son in his own likeness, after his image; and called his name Seth. . . . And all the days that Adam lived were nine hundred and thirty years; and he died.

(GEN. 5: 1-3, 5)

A resemblance to the Bible's recounting of the descendents of Adam appears in the clay prism known as the Sumerian king list (left), compiled in the second millennium B.C. and now in the Ashmolean Museum, Oxford. But, outdoing mere Biblical mortals, however longlived (Methusaleh reached the age of nine hundred and sixty-nine) this Sumerian list records legendary kings of fantastic longevity: in Eridu, A-lulim is described as ruling 28,800 years. Two kings ruled for 64,800 years. Then, we are told, "the flood swept over the earth."

And Abraham lifted up his eyes, and looked, and behold behind him a ram caught in the thicket by his horns. And Abraham went and took the ram, and offered him up for a burnt-offering in the stead of his son. . . . And because he had not withheld his son, the Lord said: I will bless thee, and multiply thy seed as the stars of heaven. . . .

(GEN. 22:13, 17)

This ram peering from the branches of a tree was found in the city of Ur, the birthplace of the patriarch Abraham. As a substitute offering for the boy Isaac, the ram was established as an important part of ancient Hebrew sacrificial ritual. This figure, adorned with gold and lapis lazuli over wood, dates from the third millennium B.C. and is now in the British Museum.

Make thee an ark of gopher wood; with rooms shalt thou make the ark, and shalt pitch it within and without with pitch. And this is how thou shalt make it: the length of the ark three hundred cubits, the breadth of it fifty cubits, and the height of it thirty cubits . . . behold, I do bring the flood of waters upon the earth to destroy all flesh. . . . But I will establish My covenant with thee.

(GEN. 6:14-15, 17-18)

The bearded man facing the calf on this ancient seal stone (above), recalls Noah and the "cattle after their kind," which the Lord commanded him to salvage from the deluge. The Biblical account parallels the Babylonian Gilgamish epic, whose hero, Ut-Napishtim, was saved from the flood by the warning of the god Ea. The seal stone carved with a small Mesopotamian river boat is in the Pergamon Museum in Berlin.

Rebekah saw Isaac, *And she said unto the servant: "What man is this that walketh in the field to meet us?" And the servant said: "It is my master." And she took her veil, and covered herself. . . . And Isaac . . . took Rebekah, and she became his wife; and he loved her.*
(GEN. 24:65, 67)

And the chief butler told his dream to Joseph, and said to him: "In my dream, behold, a vine was before me; and in the vine were three branches; and as it was budding, its blossoms shot forth, and the clusters thereof brought forth ripe grapes; and Pharaoh's cup was in my hand; and I took the grapes, and pressed them into Pharaoh's cup, and I gave the cup into Pharaoh's hand."
(GEN. 40:9–11)

These stone forms from a Palmyran relief of the first century A.D. attest to the gesture of Eastern etiquette with which Rebekah greeted the important visitor soon to be her husband. The veiling of the face also affirms Rebekah's noble origins, since the nomads of Canaan generally did not follow this custom of respect.

Colorful vintage scenes, such as this harvest (right) from the tomb of Nakht in Thebes, testify to the high development of vine-growing in ancient Egypt. This art was originally brought from Asia, and the Egyptians soon became so expert that they developed an intricate system of wine classification. The chief butler's dream of preparing Pharaoh's wine cup recalls his function as official taster before the serving of the royal meal.

Of these were the isles of the nations divided in their lands, every one after his tongue. . . . And the sons of Ham: Cush, and Mizraim, and Put, and Canaan . . . Mizraim begot Ludim, and Anamim, and Lehabim, and Naphtuhim, and Pathrusim and Cashluhim—whence went forth the Philistines—and Caphtorim. And Canaan begot Zidon his firstborn, and Heth . . . afterward were the families of the Canaanite spread abroad.
(GEN. 10:5-6, 13-15, 18)

Into the melting pot of Egypt poured the races of the ancient world. On the wall painting below from the tomb of Seti, *c.* 1300 B.C., they are distinguished by the color of their skin and their special dress. From right to left: white-skinned people of Put, or Libya, to the west; black-skinned people of Cush, or Nubia, to the south; brown-skinned people of Canaan to the east; reddish-skinned sons of Mizraim (Egypt) including the Philistines and inhabitants of Caphtor, or Crete.

And Joseph was brought down to Egypt, and Potiphar, an officer of Pharaoh's the captain of the guard, an Egyptian, bought him of the hand of the Ishmaelites, that had brought him down thither. . . . And Joseph found favor in his sight. . . . And he appointed him overseer over his house, and all that he had he put into his hand . . . the Lord blessed the Egyptian's house for Joseph's sake.

(GEN. 39:1, 4–5)

Egyptian army officers were strong silent types who wore golden necklaces and armlets, wigs and loincloths, as exemplified by this wooden statue from Thebes of the Eighteenth Dynasty presently in the Bode Museum, Berlin. Potiphar was responsible for the internal security of the palace and was also in charge of the royal prison in which Joseph was later placed when Potiphar's wife vengefully accused him of making improper advances to her.

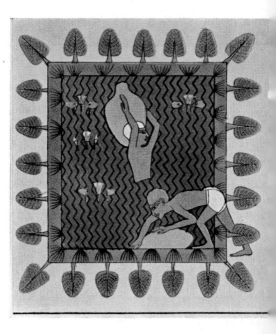

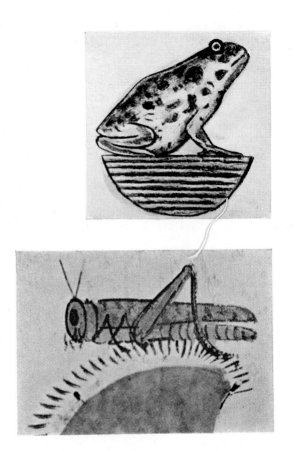

And if thou refuse to let them go, behold, I will smite all thy borders with frogs. And the river shall swarm with frogs, which shall go up and come into thy house, and into thy bedchamber . . . Behold, tomorrow will I bring locusts . . . and they shall cover the face of the earth, that one shall not be able to see the earth . . . and shall eat every tree which groweth. . . .
(EXOD. 7:27–28; 10:4–5)

Frogs and locusts are natural pests of the Nile Valley, but the story of the ten plagues assumes a vast increase to further harass the Egyptians. Divine powers were attributed to the frog, which multiplies after the yearly inundation of the Nile. Appropriately, this hieroglyphic frog sign represents Heket, goddess of childbirth and fertility. The desert locust is painted on the tomb of Horemheb at Thebes.

And the Egyptians made the children of Israel to serve with rigor. And they made their lives bitter with hard service, in mortar and in brick. . . . And the same day Pharaoh commanded the taskmasters of the people, and their officers, saying: "Ye shall no more give the people straw to make brick, as heretofore. Let them go and gather straw for themselves."
(EXOD. 1:13–14; 5:6–7)

The making of bricks in Egypt is shown on this wall painting from the tomb of Rekhmire at Thebes, fifteenth century B.C. From left to right, two men bring water from a pool to moisten the clay while others knead and carry it for shaping in brick molds. Nile mud, a combination of clay and sand, was the basic ingredient, while the straw which the Israelites sought in the fields held the clay together.

And the Egyptians pursued, and went in after them into the midst of the sea, all Pharaoh's horses, his chariots, and his horsemen. . . . And the Lord said unto Moses: "Stretch out thy hand over the sea, that the waters may come back upon the Egyptians." . . . And the waters returned, and covered the chariots, and the horsemen, even all the host of Pharaoh that went in. . . .

(EXOD. 14:23, 26, 28)

The scene of Pharaoh drawing a taut bow behind his racing steeds is a ceremonial painting from the tomb of Tutankhamon, fourteenth century B.C. It recalls the hot pursuit of the Israelites to the Red Sea when the hand of the Lord discomfited the six hundred picked chariots of the Egyptians, "took off their chariot wheels and made them drive heavily." These swift and proud chariots had been the core of Pharaoh's fighting force.

The Wreck

DRAWINGS BY GERRY GERSTEN

Remains of the status system: "a storeroom of broken monuments"

of the Status System

The widespread image of a conformist America clinging to ladders of caste is belied by the symbols of prestige that wear out, decline in power, and are then replaced. We are now freer, one critic holds, to act on our own

By ERIC LARRABEE

Americans are perennially fascinated by themselves. Perhaps this is a bad sign, if you were to measure us against Alfred North Whitehead's axiom that "a culture is in its finest flower before it begins to analyze itself." But if that is so, then we never had a flowering, for Americans have been self-conscious from the start. What is this new man? asked Hector St. Jean de Crèvecœur, and the new men have ever since been eagerly offering to tell him.

Currently the American appetite for introspection appears to be as unassuaged as always. The number one best seller has been Vance Packard's *The Status Seekers,* a book that makes us out as "badly maladjusted to our environment and becoming more maladjusted every month." Mr. Packard has examined a number of sociological studies of contemporary America, and has found a bookful of them to support his view, to wit:

> The forces of the times seem to be conspiring to squeeze individuality and spontaneity from us. We compete for the same symbols of bigness and success. We are careful to conform to the kinds of behavior approved by our peers. We are wary of others who don't look like our kind of people. We tend to judge people by their labels. And all too often we judge people on the basis of the status symbols they display.

Further evidence is not far to find. Turning to that ever-vigilant collector of cultural statistics, the *Wall Street Journal,* I discover from a recent clipping the following examples of status symbolism in action: (1) In Miami there is a flourishing business in renting furs. (2) In Detroit and Philadelphia the price of foreign cigarettes, in response to demand, has gone from 40 cents to $1.45 a pack. (3) In St.

Louis there is a good market for big game heads to be mounted on trophy room walls. And (4) a Los Angeles car dealer says he is doing well with a bronze plaque reading, "This car made especially for ———," for the dashboard of Plymouths.

Status has been discovered not only by the status-seekers, but by those shrewd and observant organizations which thrive on giving advice to industry. There is, according to the Opinion Research Corporation of Princeton, New Jersey, a "leadership elite for change" that needs only to be located by the aspiring manufacturer of a new product to make certain his success. From a study of one hundred and five families in Ridgewood, New Jersey, Opinion Research has singled out a group they call the "high mobiles," who accounted for 100 per cent of the purchases of stereo high-fidelity equipment, frozen soups, and wall-to-wall carpeting before the other laggard families—naturally known as "medium mobiles" and "low mobiles"—got into the act. The "low mobiles," on the other hand, led in the adoption of copper pots and pans, which I would regard as a sinister finding were I in the copper pot-and-pan trade.

In short, we have carried self-consciousness to the point where it is more than slightly absurd. We give the impression of a nation continually taking its own pulse. Sociology, or what passes for it, has been so popularized that its jargon has reached both market place and dinner table; the exchange of amateur observations has become a game in itself, and the discoverer of a new "status symbol" can live off it conversationally for weeks. Fashions of behavior are labeled virtually as soon as they exist, and written up

With this article HORIZON *begins a series of inquiries into the present shape and course of America's social order, and the attitudes that reflect it. Since our culture is, as Mr. Larrabee puts it, a highly self-conscious one intent on "taking its own pulse," it seems timely to examine the facts, the diagnoses, and the pulse-takers too. The next article, to appear in the January issue, will deal with the conflict between the ideals of Mass Culture and Class Culture in our midst today.*

21

The true victims of a dying status system are not the skeptics but the faithful.

in magazines, so that they become old hat for some almost before they have had time to be fashionable for others. As can be seen from the *In and Out Book,* a slender volume which tries both to ridicule and ride this trend, anything that is really *In* is automatically *Out.*

But is it all that bad? Are we as harried, stultified, and victimized as Mr. Packard says we are? He has been somewhat severely taken to task by the professionals for misrepresenting their data to support his case; and one, Seymour M. Lipset, has pointed out (in *The Reporter*) that the characteristics Mr. Packard makes the most of were noticed in Americans long before *he* came on the scene. "The image of the American conformist is prominent in the writings of Tocqueville," writes Mr. Lipset, "and Harriet Martineau reported in 1837 that 'Americans may travel over the world, and find no society but their own which will submit [as much] to the restraint of perpetual caution, and reference to the opinions of others.'"

Mr. Packard's avowed purpose is admirable. He is filled with despair at the prospect he describes, and he has described it precisely in the hope that something can be done—something to save the values of individual worth, initiative, and opportunity before they are swallowed up in snobbery, emulation, and caste. But he has chosen to do this by painting the picture black, blacker indeed than it is; and there is a danger here that the method will defeat itself and backfire. Better to be realistic, even at the cost of having to admit one is well off, than to magnify the nightmare for the sake of its salutary effect. There are enough real nightmares.

Actually we are living not so much in a status system as in the wreckage of one, a storeroom full of broken monuments; for the process of exploiting status is self-destructive, and ruins each new idol that it raises. Once commerce gets its greasy fingers on a class distinction there is little enough left of it; and given the effort and incentive there is no honor, no eminence, no ornament that cannot be cheapened and coarsened and marketed to the millions. A hierarchy subject to merchandising is no longer binding on the independent individual—and this is what saves us.

The shell of the status system which we occupy can even now, admittedly, do damage to those unfortunates who go astray among its dingy, shattered statuary. But no one is

required to. No one is compelled to engage in the bootless pursuit of symbols that have lost their meaning, or to keep up with Joneses who are merely seeking to keep up. The ordeal of competitive consumption is not mandatory, and there are many alternatives for those who can replace the search for pseudo-symbols with the search for something else —for competence, or merely for pleasure, or for some Grail of their own contriving. We are not condemned to take the worn-out system seriously; and its true victims are not the skeptics but the faithful, those who haven't yet seen the flaw within the marble, and still believe in the fallen gods.

The idea of social class is one of the most useful, and most risky, weapons in the armory of the social scientist. It has enormous plausibility. We all know that "class" exists, and we are continually confronted with evidences of it. Moreover, the more "scientific" of the life sciences, like biology, have passed this way before—and attained their present levels of reliability—by beginning with the Linnaean, or classifying, stage and dividing the raw material for study into families and species.

Once you have assumed that there is such a thing as "class," proofs of its existence follow with gratifying ease. Income levels distribute themselves across a workable scale; styles of living show welcome contrasts; and individuals turn out to judge one another's "place" with a satisfactory degree of unanimity. Obviously many people do not stay in place, and this leads to the equally plausible idea of "mobility," or moving from class to class—the unstable quality that presumably made the "high mobiles" in Ridgewood so vulnerable to stereo, soup, and carpets. On this theoretical skeleton can be hung a structure as complicated as the investigator desires, as adaptable to primitive tribes as to the status-graders of a modern industry. Like all self-confirming propositions, however, it is less useful than it looks.

For example, one of the modern sociologists who has leaned heavily on the idea of "class" is W. Lloyd Warner, whose Yankee City Series has handled a New England community on the hypothesis that it is composed of six classes: upper-upper, lower-upper, upper-middle, lower-middle, upper-lower, and lower-lower. Warner uses what can be called the "subjective" rather than the "objective" meaning of the

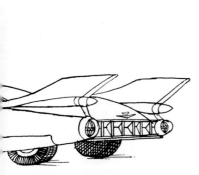

There is always some joker, as the Navy adage holds, who doesn't get the word

word "class"—that is, he is more concerned with the classes people think they belong to, or are assigned to by others, than he is with the class they would be placed in by income or by some other tangible factor. Warner argues, nonetheless, that his classes do in actuality exist, encompassing both meanings, and this has led some of his colleagues to complain. For instance, it has prompted C. Wright Mills (author of *White Collar* and *The Power Elite*) to insist that a good definition should be one-dimensional, so that you can make it hold still while other variables move; but Mills thinks that in Warner's hands the word "class" has become what he calls a "sponge word," so filled with various notions that you can never be sure which one you're dealing with. Mills would much prefer to define "class" in financial or similarly objective terms, and set aside the word "status" for the far less precise impressions that people have about each other, and themselves.

Yet even with this division of labor between the words, "status" is still a source of difficulty. The elements that make it up can be scored on an I.S.C., or Index of Status Characteristics, yet these will often differ from place to place, or even from time to time. One is hard put to demonstrate that status is *there,* inherent in the situation, and not brought along by the investigator in the baggage of his preconceptions. In such circumstances the test of an idea is not how sensible it seems, but how effective it is in solving problems that could not otherwise be posed. If "status" is simply a name for what we already know by other means, then its use will beg all the questions that we ought to be asking: what is it? how do we know? what creates it? what consequences follow? The sociologists themselves are in good part aware of this, and they handle their terminology—clumsy as it is—with a certain restraint. But in the process of converting to layman's language, many of the reservations and caveats get lost; and the results are subsequently served up to the public, with a spurious and unintended authority, as the pronouncements of social science.

"Status" has still another hold on the public imagination, derived from the parlor-game fascination that comes of putting people in pigeonholes; and this has been formidably strengthened by the recent emergence, during these postwar years, of a school of amateur and unofficial sociology, staffed mainly by journalists and dedicated to the proposition that one man's "insight" is as good as another's. Postwar prosperity brought with it an unprecedented opportunity for American self-consciousness to expand and exercise itself. When the late forties came we looked at one another with wild surmise and saw much that fell into patterns—like Madison Avenue, button-down shirts, grey flannel suits—and there were satisfactions to be had in naming the new categories, and guessing where one stood in them oneself.

The late Professor Irwin Edman of Columbia, who deplored the tendency, spoke of its exponents as "anthropologists without portfolio." Perhaps I exaggerate in using the word "school," since they had so little in common; but it has always seemed to me that these writers, no matter how far apart they appeared to be, were responding to a similar need—for accurate descriptions of how we truly behave as a means of liberation from the dead hand of obsolete stereotypes that were no longer relevant. In that respect what Russell Lynes was doing for taste, Stephen Potter for "gamesmanship," John K. Galbraith for economics, Alfred C. Kinsey for sex, William H. Whyte, Jr., for the suburbs, Samuel Lubell for politics, Cleveland Amory for "society," or David Riesman for Academia had more in common than appeared. It was a great period for giving conferences, which might be called the Group Therapy Method of trying to find out who we are—or trying, as Margaret Mead put it at a conference in 1951, "to make self-consciousness *bearable* to Americans."

Note further that none of these observers of the passing scene was neutral; they also shared an awareness that pointing out a behavior pattern is a moral act, and that they themselves, like it or not, were moralists. Social science proper, in the effort to ape the natural sciences, has too long tended to be manipulative without being responsible; that is, to make a goal for its own sake of predicting and controlling human beings as though they were molecules, without regard to aims and outcomes. Fortunately there is a countervailing force, which David Riesman especially embodies, directed toward the old-fashioned object of enlightening people in order to emancipate them, not least from their own personalities. We are a mixed product, not only of status and the other social sanctions, but of the character and identities we have chosen for ourselves; and often we are as much imprisoned by the latter as the former.

THE AMERICA OF W. LLOYD WARNER

Studying his country today, the sociologist W. Lloyd Warner sees a six-tiered society which resembles many a northeastern mill town, rising from the factories and slums by the river through middle-class neighborhoods to the house of the old, established family on the hill. In a series of volumes on "Yankee City" (Newburyport, Massachusetts) he has labeled and defined his levels of class: the upper-upper, at the peak of long-standing prestige; the lower-upper, who have wealth but acquired it too recently; the upper-middle, "solid citizens" who play a major role in civic life; the lower-middle, the top level of the Common Man, small businessmen likely to be members of the fraternal orders; the upper-lower, the "honest" workman and small tradesman, who are still respectable; and finally the lower-lower, at the bottom of the heap, where newly arrived ethnic groups are just beginning their ascent.

Warner recognizes that this pattern does not prevail everywhere in the United States. Especially in the West and Southwest, there are proportionately fewer persons to be found in the top and bottom tiers. Many American cities are not yet old enough for "old families" to have achieved that privileged status, and many have not received the influx of immigrants which is necessary to replenish the bottom row.

But in general he argues that an American class system does exist, so that people can migrate from one region to another, still recognize their own level, and move comfortably within it. In "Yankee City" the largest single class is the upper-lower, accounting for a third of the total population. Both the lower-lower and the lower-middle take up about a quarter apiece, leaving a tenth for the upper-middle and scarcely a fifteenth for the top two levels combined.

Individuals are located in Warner's class system by an Index of Status Characteristics in which four factors are given a weighted value: occupation counts four, source of income and type of house count three apiece, and neighborhood counts two. Each of the factors is rated on a scale of 1 (high) to 7 (low), so that top score is 7 and bottom is 84. If you are a salaried clerk, living in an average-sized house in a neighborhood slightly on the downgrade, Warner's tabulation would establish that you are definitely lower-middle class—which is perhaps why sociologists are sometimes accused of seeking complicated methods to prove the self-evident.

Yet Warner believes that a status system is in fact desirable for a society to have. "The principle of rank and status," he writes, "is necessary to provide men with the motives to excel by striving for positions of higher prestige and power for themselves and for their families. It is also essential to equip the nation, communities, and their institutions with responsible leadership hierarchies which co-ordinate and regulate the lives of their inhabitants and help maintain an orderly way of life, in which their citizens can cultivate the morals and manners of a high civilization."

Satire and social commentary have the redeeming function of lifting us out of the "given," the morass of roles and habits—satire's natural target—which we normally inhabit. A "humorist" like Stephen Potter not only has the malicious pleasure of revealing frauds and pretensions for what they are, but he is also saying in effect, "If there is no more to you than this, this bundle of devices for being 'one-up' that my books describe, then you deserve to be laughed at." Russell Lynes, similarly, in his notable magazine article called "Highbrow, Lowbrow, Middlebrow," was showing that at each of these three status-levels of taste it is possible to fake—to own the right objects and say the right things, automatically, with only the most casual comprehension of them—and the moral was there for anyone to read: only if you do not fake, and listen quietly to what your psyche tells you, can you be wholly unafraid.

"Status," in other words, has been enjoying a factitious popularity. The professional sociologists need more than this term to explain how society functions, and many of them are far from satisfied with it. Doubtless a generation has come along that is hypersensitive to status, and saturated in the semiacademic vocabulary. ("We don't mind it here," a young couple told me once in Levittown, Pennsylvania. "We're project-oriented.") But the system cuts both ways. To describe it is to call it into question; why abide by it if you know how it works? A shelfful of books has prepared the way for Vance Packard, but they do not support him; for many have pictured the masks we wear, as he has, only to make us uncomfortable, and many have reminded us, in louder tones than his, that there is no alternative to the Self.

It will be argued, if the objections occurring to me occur to anyone else, that all this applies only to an intelligent minority of Americans, a minority within the already small minority who know that Vance Packard is an author. A far larger number, you will say, are still engaged in the indefatigable pursuit of all the status symbols they can lay their hands on, and they show no signs of slackening. Maybe so, but let us look then at the circumstances in which they run this mournful race, and the forces which conspire to frustrate them. It is not to the swift, nor are the prizes—the external symbols of status—made of pure metal. They change quickly and are subject, as the winner of them may discover, to sudden devaluation.

Let us confess that in our most favored country the Great Game of Consumption has become a free-for-all. We have an economy based on the Keynesian principle that everyone should consume, to keep the wheels of mass production turning; and we have reconciled ourselves to taxes and subsidies that buoy up some classes, and drag down others, until all are brought within the limits of the Game, and made subject to its rules. These require that everyone should seek to replace whatever he owns with something better, thus moving up the ladder of status; yet they require also that the objects available should become more and more alike, so that the ladder gets shorter and shorter, and the incentives to climb it diminish in proportion. And here the best of status systems fail.

Consider the manufacture that has done more than any other to put status on a paying basis: namely, automobiles. This was the industry in which mass production reached its earliest and fullest flowering, where the opportunity first arose to give the customer more than he wanted—the intangibles of style, convenience, and self-satisfaction. The auto makers learned, and other industrialists have learned it from them, how to use the added increment of symbolism to make the difference between a passably successful product and one that sells in quantity. The automobile was not simply an automobile; it was an expression of power, of sex, and of prestige. It became the status symbol par excellence: "If you've earned it," read the Cadillac advertisements, in magnificent simplicity, "why hesitate?"

Then mass production began to work its homogenizing magic. Once there had been many makes of cars, many levels of ownership. Gradually they had shaken down to the so-called lower-, medium-, and upper-price ranges; but even this was too much for a status-hungry market. There was a totem pole, but nobody wanted to be low man. One by one the lower-price cars became longer, beefier, faster, and fancier; until soon there was no such thing as the "medium-price" range, and a grandiose effort to invade it—by the Edsel—fell resoundingly on its face. Where once there had been a recognizable ladder, there was now an undifferentiated blur. "Why buy a Buick," ran the Detroit jibe, "when for two hundred dollars more you can get a Chevrolet?"

This would be of no great importance, except that it is a portent. Concurrently with the disintegration of the automotive ranking system, a large number of customers were indicating that they simply wanted no part of it. Money that used to go into the difference between a Detroit automobile and a functional means of transportation was now going elsewhere: into boats, swimming pools, winter vacations, elaborate sports equipment or, most scandalous of all, Volkswagens. The foreign car—which Detroit at first sneered at, explained away, and then proceeded to imitate—is a perfect example of the device which can take over when a status system dies. It was a way of clearing the board, of saying, "Thanks just the same, but I won't play any more."

Thus always with tyrants. There is no safety in status when everyone else is after the same thing and, what is more, can get it. One by one the symbols will exhaust themselves, and be replaced by others, until someday a less gregarious and antagonistic animal replaces us. "A $6000 pool is no longer a high-status symbol," according to an official of the National Swimming Pool Institute. "You must spend another $6000 for trimmings such as cabana, bar, patio, exotic landscaping. Free-form and kidney pools are so common they mean nothing. Now you must have the shape of a cowboy boot or the state of Florida even to be noticed."

CONTINUED ON PAGE 128

THE AMERICA OF C. WRIGHT MILLS

C. Wright Mills is the caustic critic of an America far removed from the tree-lined streets of Warner's "Yankee City." His world is metropolitan, seen through the grey haze of the 1930's; and rather than accept Warner's six classes he has chosen to concentrate on two, devoting a book to each—*White Collar* (1951) and *The Power Elite* (1956). To him the twentieth century is the period par excellence of the middle class, which has slipped half-consciously into historical prominence without any sense of organized identity, without continuity with the past, without control over the future. Power, with which Mills is much concerned, resides elsewhere—in the "power elite."

It is typical of the American elite, so Mills says, that they tend to deny being powerful. Yet the characteristic of this group is its ability to make significant decisions in a society where, for the vast majority, individual decisions do not count. The "power elite" are the men who occupy pivotal positions in the hierarchy —part industrial, part military, part political—which determines, in Mills's view, the essential shape and substance of modern life. They are the managing directors, the public figures, the generals and admirals (and, mingling with them, "those professional celebrities who live by being continually displayed"), and they are also, Mills allows, people of sufficient character and energy to transcend the "white collar" existence.

To our somber, bourgeois lives Mills devotes his most biting commentary, for the troubles of the American middle class—so he argues—will soon be those of men and women everywhere. "What must be grasped is the picture of society as a great salesroom, an enormous file, an incorporated brain, a new universe of management and manipulation." There are now four times as many wage-and-salary earners as there are independent entrepreneurs, and we are continually inventing new professions to build out the roster—new kinds of hired bureaucrats, captive technicians, "social engineers," or girl Fridays. Thus a new class has been created, aware of social change but unable to influence it— "people," in Mills's words, "who have been stood up by life; what they most desire is forbidden them by reason of what they are."

Mills's White Collar Man—with no golden age, no plan of life, no culture to lean on—is pushed by forces beyond his control into movements he does not understand. He makes excellent material for the synthetic molding of his motives by mass media, and is especially vulnerable to their onslaught of manufactured loyalties and distractions. White-collar workers may vie with one another in emulating models of behavior just beyond their reach, but satisfaction is short-lived; on the job no status is secure, each hurdle has another one beyond it, and the symbols of each new step upward, having been savored in advance, lose their flavor when attained. The result Mills calls the "Status Panic," an inevitably frustrating struggle to find one's self in a "market of strangers," where evidences of prestige are fragile and fleeting, and all dreams are false.

25

By ROBERT EMMETT GINNA

Our man from New York

observes

Carol Reed

directing

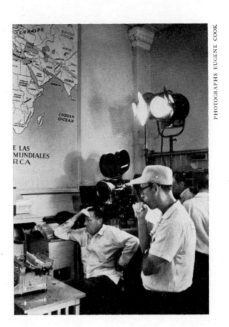

"OUR MAN IN HAVANA"

Inside the cable office, on Calle Obispo in the heart of Old Havana, an exhibition bizarre enough to delight a surrealist's eye was in progress. Into the cramped office during the height of business tramped an army of movie technicians. Through the building, around columns, between teletype machines, they strung a maze of cable. Over the workers' desks they erected a battery of lights that lit and heated the premises like an inferno. Meanwhile the Cuban operators, file clerks, and messengers carried on as usual, hammering out messages, stepping over and around obstacles, smoking their long, black after-lunch cigars. I should have thought I was an onlooker at a Marx Brothers extravaganza with twenty-two Grouchos loping about for good measure, had I not recognized the tall man ambling nonchalantly about through the mess, waiting to get on with his film-making when the technical chiefs reported that they were ready. Sir Carol Reed, one of the cinema's masters, was about to direct a scene from Graham Greene's *Our Man in Havana*.

The shot they had to make could not have been simpler. It

A man with a reputation for unruffled calm, Sir Carol Reed (left) nonetheless runs the gamut of emotions from intense animation to deep contemplation (above), while directing a scene in a cable office during the filming of Our Man in Havana.

required an operator to take an incoming cable from a spindle, note that it was in code, then surreptitiously type a copy of it. This fragment would fit into a montage designed to indicate that a network of unidentified spies was moving against the British hero-spy of the story. The shot would not run more than a few seconds in the montage. A regular cable operator, not an actor, was to play the role. Before starting to film, Sir Carol summoned the operator, and through an interpreter explained the action expected of him. But Sir Carol did not leave the explanation at that. He told the operator the entire story of the film, with particulars of every character and where they fitted into it. Finally he emphasized that the scene would run but fifteen seconds in the finished film; thus every movement of the hands and eyes must convey the point. When he had finished, he asked for a rehearsal. The operator went through the action. Pleased, clapping his hands, Reed called out, "Let's film it."

The operator took his place, the camera was set in motion, the man picked up the cable form, glanced around, then hurriedly copied it, his every motion and attitude precisely as the director had asked. Reed consulted his cameramen. They reported that all was correct from their end. "Fine. That's it then," said the director with a tired, satisfied sigh, doubtless feeling in his heart that he had done everything possible

27

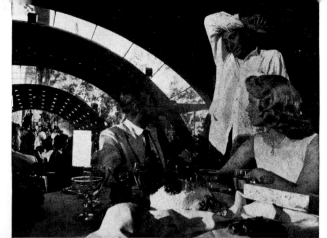

With Carol Reed in Havana: "If anyone thinks directing is easy . . ."

During the location work for Our Man in Havana *Sir Carol Reed rehearses his actors for a key scene. Above, while the stars Burl Ives and Sir Alec Guinness sit at a table in the garish Tropicana casino that is to provide the setting, he instructs ingénue Jo Morrow in what he wants. The screenplay describes a birthday dinner given by the movie's hero-spy (Guinness) for his daughter (Jo Morrow) in the presence of the old family friend (Ives), who later sells the hero out to other spies. In the two stars Reed had adroit performers, able to govern the shading of their play as with a rheostat. In Miss Morrow he had the story-book image of a Hollywood starlet. The play between the actors had to be subtle; the audience must sense that Ives is getting a clue to Guinness's espionage through Miss Morrow's inadvertent remarks. Left, after a "take" Reed continues to struggle to get precisely what he wants from Miss Morrow. Finally (right) the scene is done, leaving him limp and prayerful.*

PHOTOGRAPHS EUGENE COOK

The term "director's touch" is one bandied about film circles. Although Sir Carol Reed says he is unsure what it means, most film people use it in referring to some device by which the director either symbolizes the film's theme or solves a complicated problem shot. The "director's touch" was everywhere evident as Reed filmed Our Man in Havana. On a street (above, left) he directs the two Cuban players whose silent love story he has threaded throughout the film as a shadowy subordinate theme. In a doorway he pauses with stars Maureen O'Hara and Alec Guinness (above, right), suggesting that in the next scene she stop to fix her heel during a stroll, thus making it possible to record their dialogue in close-up, and avoiding a difficult "tracking shot." On the steps of a precinct police station where the crew lunched daily (below), he goes over a tricky scene with the two stars and the script-girl. On the left, some members of Fidel Castro's new police pass by.

to make that moment tell in the over-all fabric of his film.

The novel Sir Carol had chosen to film is not one of Graham Greene's best. It is itself not quite a thriller like Greene's earlier books, nor does it have the depth of insight which marks the author's serious books about mortals tormented with the problems set by Heaven. It is one of those works which Greene frankly calls "an entertainment." It has Greene's nice observations, his penetrations beneath the surface of events, and a choice assemblage of characters.

Carol Reed is an old hand with spies and derring-do. Things crackle in his pictures: his best ones (*Night Train, Odd Man Out, The Third Man*) are studies of vivid characters enmeshed in situations of great tension, hurtling along like the Orient Express. Now, seeing his touch and listening to his summation of the story, I sensed that the film would be more effective than the novel.

Its hero is a man named Wormold (who was to be portrayed by Sir Alec Guinness). He is the Cuban representative of a British vacuum cleaner manufacturer. He is himself English, middle-aged, cast off by his wife for another; a proper, circumspect man in a city that offers every inducement for the European to go to seed—women, rum, easy ways—all of them cheap. Wormold's life orbits about his seventeen-year-old daughter, Milly (played by Jo Morrow). His one good friend is an aging German physician named Hasselbacher (Burl Ives), who dispenses shrewd philosophy over their daily daiquiris. Into this uneventful life simultaneously intrude two dangerous forces. One is Captain Segura of the Secret Police of the Batista regime, who carries a cigarette case made of human skin and is known as The Red Vulture. Segura (Ernie Kovacs) takes a fancy to Milly. Just as Wormold is despairing of getting Milly away from Segura and safely off to school in Switzerland, a fastidious stranger named Hawthorne (Noel Coward) appears. In the men's room of Sloppy Joe's, Hawthorne commences to recruit Wormold into the British Secret Service. Moved by the double appeal of loyalty and enough money to raise his daughter properly, Wormold becomes a spy. Hawthorne goes back to London and reports to his frosty chief (Sir Ralph Richardson) that their man in Havana, Agent 59200/5, is a reliable type of businessman with the best connections.

To nourish the thirst for information at headquarters, Wormold conceives an elaborate deception. He devises drawings based on his firm's new "Atomic Pile Cleaner," and, blowing them up overscale, sends them to London as the plans of top secret works being installed by Cubans in the mountains of Oriente province. London dispatches a trained team, a codist (Maureen O'Hara) and a radioman, to assist him. The game turns rough when real spies—The Others—intervene. By blackmail they force Dr. Hasselbacher to betray Wormold, then kill the old man. In short order the mild Wormold has killed the chief enemy agent, and Segura has informed the British Secret Service of Wormold's fraud. Mr. Greene concludes his spoof with a delicious scene in London, in which the Chief stiffly informs the frightened Wormold, who is prepared for punishment, that he is to be decorated and kept on as an instructor. It is clear that the Secret Service has decided it dare not let the intelligence branches of the military services know it has been duped. However slight the story, all the ingredients for an Alec Guinness romp are here.

When the episode in the cable office was completed, night had settled over Havana. As I drove along the magnificent Malecón bordering the Gulf, the great number of strollers on the sea wall and the strains of music floating with the fragrant tropic odors on the air lent the capital an aura of ease and gaiety at variance with the appearance of Fidel Castro's wretched-looking soldiery, who were deployed everywhere. A note of that illogical puritanism that has frequently distinguished revolutions was reflected in the shuttered windows of the poorer bordellos, while the flossiest beckoned with its neon lights. My destination was the Hotel Capri, a glittering slice of pink-and-white hotel confectionery, where the principal personages of the motion picture company were established.

I located Sir Carol Reed standing amid a group, his height and sure, authoritative bearing distinctive. He suggested that we sit down to talk in the lobby of the hotel. I could not have imagined a less desirable place for a conversation, but the director was able to concentrate completely, ignoring the gaily plumaged birds passing in and out of the casino just off the lobby.

I began by asking about the director's contribution to the screenplay that Graham Greene had fashioned from his novel. "This is our third collaboration," said Sir Carol. "We came to Havana for two weeks last October to pick locations. And do you know, Graham predicted everything that has happened. I was worried about how the old regime would react to the nasty suggestions about them in the book, but he said, 'Don't worry, they'll be all washed up by the time we're ready to come back here for production.' After soaking up the feel of the place for a couple of weeks we went back to Brighton and dug in. We spent five weeks in a quiet place, Graham in one room, I in the next. He would write from 8 A.M. to 7 P.M. with time out for beer and sandwiches. We'd talk over progress at dinner, try out ideas. Then with a first draft of the script done, we went to Cádiz in Spain because it has something of the color and waterfront feel of Havana. We worked there for a few weeks, then went to London to put the finishing touches on the script."

"The quality I find most striking about your movies is their pace," I said. "They seem to gather momentum as they move along. Is this pace something you build into the picture while filming it, or later, when cutting it?"

"Both, of course. Following the picture through to the last detail is critical, terribly important," he said. "You know, not enough directors are willing to do this. They are too eager to run off and play in the south of France—they want their money fast and easy. As soon as shooting is over, they're

CONTINUED ON PAGE 122

31

By JOHN RUSSELL
ART CRITIC OF THE LONDON *Sunday Times*

BOIGONTIER—USIS

The "New American Painting" Captures Europe

While they may baffle most of their own countrymen, innovators of the

Abstract Expressionist school are being debated and widely accepted by an

international art world that until recently disdained American painting

As far back as 1941 the European art world began hearing of something labeled "The New American Painting." Readers of Cyril Connolly's *Horizon** learned from John Rothenstein of a *levée en masse* of transatlantic artists which was likely to have extraordinary results of one sort or another; but they sat back and laughed, nonetheless, at the unnamed critic, quoted by Rothenstein, who had said that "America today is developing a school of painting which promises to be the most important movement in the world of art since the Italian Renaissance."

In England our first real intimation of the scope and stature of the new American school came, I think, in an article, again in the English *Horizon,* by Denys Sutton, lately returned from a year's lecturing at Yale. In "The Challenge of American Art," published in October, 1949, Mr. Sutton gave a vivid account, not merely of Pollock, Baziotes, Tobey, Rothko, and other abstract painters, but of the environment in which their work had been conceived. Readers learned, for instance, of how "The Museum of Modern Art has become more than a picture gallery; it is almost a club, a secret society. It is a symbol of youth, adventure and liberation. It recalls the Ibsenism of a past generation." And Mr. Sutton put for the first time two questions which were to become familiar: "Do artistic movements exist in America which may be considered on an equal footing with those of

TEXT CONTINUED ON PAGE 41

*An English magazine, edited with great distinction by Mr. Connolly between 1940 and 1950. It ceased publication eight years before the American HORIZON came into existence.

FOLLOWING: A PORTFOLIO IN GRAVURE OF NEW AMERICAN PAINTINGS RECENTLY
SHOWN IN EUROPE BEGINNING WITH SAM FRANCIS: BLUE AND BLACK (1954)

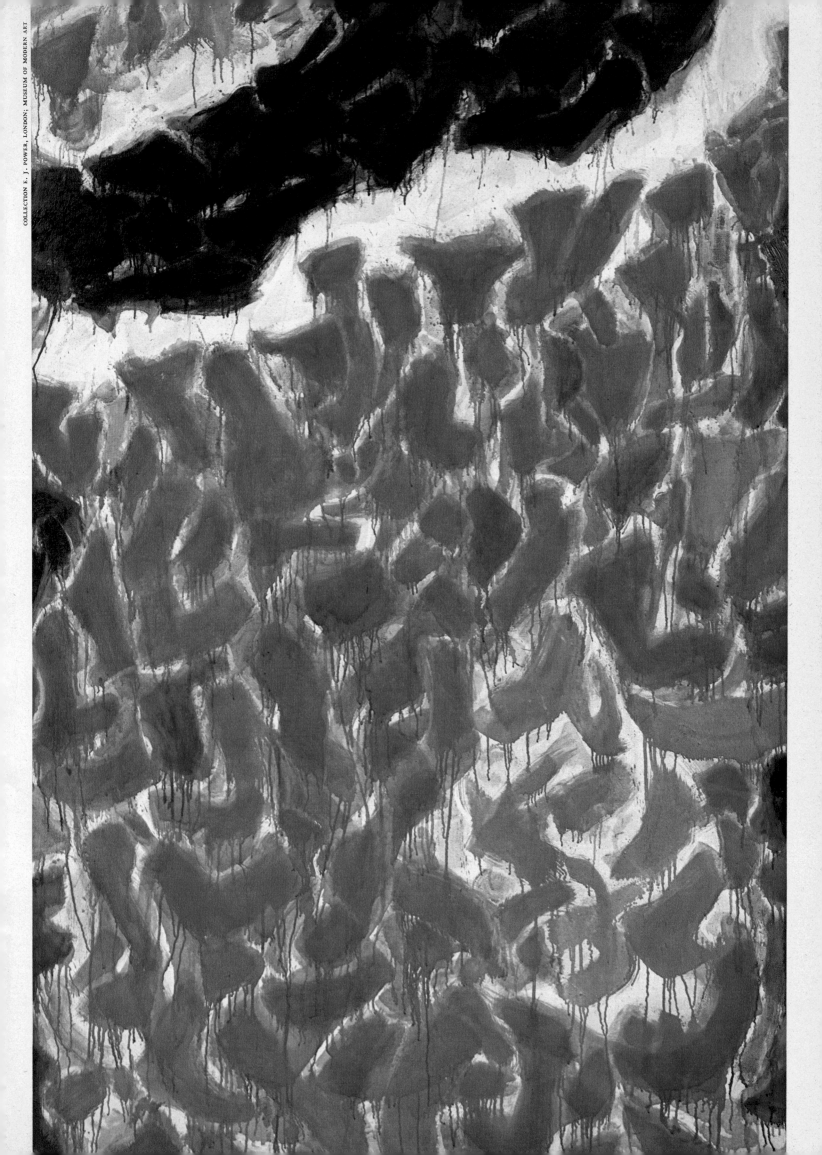

PHILIP GUSTON: THE RETURN (1956-59)

MARK ROTHKO: EARTH AND GREEN (1954-55)

JACKSON POLLOCK: ONE (1950)

ROBERT MOTHERWELL: THE VOYAGE (1949)

ADOLPH GOTTLIEB: SIDE PULL (1956)

THE ART
and the ARTISTS

The paintings in the preceding portfolio are representative works by seven American artists who have made the strongest impression abroad. Generally devoid of realistic content, such paintings are peculiarly dependent for their impact on texture and size (the Pollock, for example, measures approximately 9 by 18 feet). HORIZON therefore presents them in gravure, which gives the best reproduction of texture, and has turned several of the paintings sideways to permit a larger scale.

SAM FRANCIS, 36 (shown at work on page 32), is a Californian who lives in Paris. He spreads over his huge canvases a loose mosaic of leaflike shapes that sometimes burn like coals, sometimes gleam like petals. *Blue and Black* is owned by the prominent London collector E. J. Power.

PHILIP GUSTON, 47, was born in Canada, grew up in Los Angeles, and made a considerable reputation as a realist before turning to abstract expressionism about 1950. In his most characteristic vein he seems to pull knots of intense, ecstatic color out of a pale but echoing background.

MARK ROTHKO, 56, left Russia at the age of ten and grew up in Oregon. Once an expressionist, he has evolved his present unmistakable style during the past decade. His misty rectangles of color, glimmering like luminous fogs, express every mood from lyric calm to glowering hostility.

JACKSON POLLOCK, who died in 1956, was the greatest innovator among the new American painters and the most influential abroad. Originally a social realist, in 1947 he invented the drip technique that gives his vast paintings their seething, ceaseless movement and limitless depths.

ROBERT MOTHERWELL, 44, is a serious student of philosophy, and his paintings reflect the control of a disciplined intellect. His ochreous colors recall California, where he grew up, and Spain, which haunts much of his work (including a series of "Elegies for the Spanish Republic").

ADOLPH GOTTLIEB, 56, is a native New Yorker who experimented with primitive symbols and archaic pictographs before arriving at his current abstract idiom. His latest paintings suggest a kind of frozen instability—as in *Side Pull*, with its graphic tug-of-war between opposing forces.

GRACE HARTIGAN, 37, has said that she does not try to "describe" her subject matter but to "distill it until I have its essence." *City Life* is a distillation of the forms and colors of a New York sidewalk market—its piled-up fruits and vegetables, striped awning, and continuous bustle.

TEXT CONTINUED FROM PAGE 32

Paris, London, and Rome? Must we now look to New York in the same way as that city looked to Europe?" He left us readers to draw our own conclusions; but there was no doubt that an attentive reader would have said "Yes."

It took a long time, all the same, for even a small minority of assenters to emerge. Readjustment is always painful, and the overthrow of accepted ideas is the more difficult when those ideas carry with them associations of money-making, self-esteem, and national prestige. To accept the implications of the "New American Painting" means, for many Europeans, not so much the extension as the annihilation of a world picture which they may have been building for a lifetime; and, to those intimately concerned with art, as painters, dealers, collectors, critics, and historians, it may bring with it intimations of personal collapse. It is not remarkable that rational assessments of the new school should even now be rare; rejection on the one hand, and acceptance on the other, tend to be total, blind, unthinking.

It is only within the last few years that Europeans have been able to see many of the new American paintings in exhibitions. Some of these, and especially the "New American Painting" traveling show recently sponsored by New York's Museum of Modern Art, had a majesty of presentation which forced them upon the notice even of those who would otherwise never have been coaxed out of their insularity. Others were owed to the enthusiasm of a dealer, or of a pioneering body such as the London Institute of Contemporary Arts.

Of all the activities now open to a grown man, one of the most dispiriting is the perusal of day-to-day art criticism. Much as the verbiage collector would delight in a literal rendering of some of the European reviews, with their talk of "genesiacal incandescence" and the "impossibility of desapercibirsing a manifestation such as this," it will be more profitable to turn to some of the Europeans whose stature as artists, or dealers, or collectors, or critics has been enhanced by contact with the new American painting.

One of the best-known examples is E. J. Power, the English collector whose holdings both of *art autre* and of the new American painting were begun well ahead of fashion. There is nothing in his personal history of the traditional collector's background. Social history and philosophy were the interests by way of which he came to art; and he studied them not in the moss-grown quadrangles of Oxford or Cambridge, nor in the "book-lined study" of conservative legend, but afloat on the high seas, during long spells of service in the merchant navy. These allowed him to examine *in situ* many prodigies of ancient or primitive art which only later became familiar, through illustrated books, to his fellow collectors. Art is, to Mr. Power, the surest indicator of the condition of any given society. Where others seal it off as a mark of superiority or springboard to the "higher life" with which museums are concerned, Mr. Power sees it as environmental: a part, that is to say, of the life about him—but a part that is unusually, and sometimes uniquely, revealing. Power

CONTINUED ON PAGE 120

THE LOST MINARET OF JHAM

In a mountain valley of Afghanistan a French explorer discovered this ancient Ghorid tower, known only to legend

Deep in the valley of Jham in central Afghanistan rushes the river of Hari Rud, whose winding course for centuries led conquerors and adventurers eastward in search of new worlds. To the north in ancient Bactria, the "mother of cities," Zoroaster preached the supremacy of one God thousands of years ago. It was here and in Gandhara to the south that the Macedonian warriors of Alexander the Great molded a Graeco-Buddhist culture and left a legacy of form to the first Buddha image—that of a Greek god. Into this caldron of ideologies, in the seventh century A.D. swept the power of Islam.

The minaret of Jham, standing beside the Hari Rud, testifies to the strength of the Moslem empire by the twelfth century, when the princes of ancient Ghor built this funerary monument. Soaring 200 feet high, the minaret is a stone tower covered with decorative panels and Kufic inscription. But the strangest thing about it is that no traveler from the outside world had reported seeing it

and no one knew for sure that it existed until August, 1957, when André Maricq, a member of the French Archaeological Delegation in Afghanistan, was drawn to Ghor by the local legend of a great minaret. By car and then by horseback he descended the valley of the Jham river to its junction with the Hari Rud. Of his first sight of the minaret M. Maricq writes:

My surprise was complete. The lack of descriptive power in those who were my sources of information was such that I had been expecting a ruin rather than an intact building. At the confluence of the torrent and the river, in the midst of a circle of somber mountains, stood the golden silhouette of a colossal tower, heightened with a band of blue faience (*kashi*).

The monument rises from an octagonal base supporting three superimposed shafts in the form of truncated cones.

At the top of the first two stages, projected balconies which are now destroyed, while the third is crowned with a lantern now lacking its cover. Four great bands of Kufic break the thrust of the vertical elements and give weight to the building.

Within a year the news of M. Maricq's discovery led an English traveler, Michael Alexander, to visit the site, where he made a second discovery:

I entered the minaret, which is in a remarkable state of preservation, by a narrow aperture about 12 feet from the ground, at which point the walls are seven feet thick and constructed of flat fired bricks, about two inches high and eight inches square. A spiral staircase leads to a vaulted platform through which I passed to the second stage. Steplike bricks projecting from the side of the drum lead through other platforms and enabled me to climb to within a few feet of the top. Descending, I was surprised to find that I came to a different aperture to that by which I had entered. It was twice as far from the ground! I had to return before I solved the mystery—there were two spiral staircases. It must have been an advanced architectural problem to fit them into so narrow a shaft.

The inscription on the blue *kashis* extols the name of the great Ghorid sultan, "The august king of kings Ghiyath ud-Din Abu'l Fath, glorifier of Islam and the faithful, companion of the Emir of the faithful." It was this sultan who from his mountain fastness sent a swift and overpowering army in 1193 for the conquest of Delhi in India and whose dynasty, for a brief span of years, ruled an empire extending from the farthest reaches of India to the borders of Babylonia. M. Maricq, who has found the rubble of a sizable city near the great minaret, supposes that it marks the site of the lost Ghor capital of Firuzkoh.

By KERMIT LANSNER

olivetti: a man and a style

Typewriters, typography, model factories, showrooms—all that bears his name reflects the

advanced taste of this Italian businessman who is also a writer, publisher, and visionary

In this age of specialization the Italian Adriano Olivetti would be an extraordinary man through the sheer range of his interests. The world knows him as his country's typewriter king; he is also a writer, a patron of writers and painters, a book and magazine publisher, a social reformer and political theorist, the founder of his own political party, and today, that party's one elected representative in the Italian parliament. Yet amid this phenomenal spread of activity, much of it hardheaded and some widely looked upon as somewhat headstrong if not foot-loose, his greatest European individuality lies in one fact. It is that he combines an imaginative social sense in going about building his machines with an even more imaginative sense of design in shaping and selling them.

There are few major urban centers one can visit today without seeing the stamp of Olivetti: the suave typewriters and calculating machines that are the nearest thing to mass-produced applied sculpture we have; the brilliantly conceived

Adriano Olivetti stands before a decorative frieze of his company's factories in Europe and South America. The frieze, used on advertisements, was designed by Giovanni Pintori.

posters and advertisements that market them; and the dramatic showrooms, given form by leading designers, painters, and sculptors, that present them. In his own country, Olivetti has supplemented his major showcases with several hundred smaller ones strung up and down the peninsula; he has built new factories designed by the most adventurous architects, and he has given substance to these gleaming structures by developing a social program for his workers which is second to none in Europe. He does not speak idly when he insists that "buildings and people are the most important things in a factory. The balance sheet comes from them."

When compared with America's corporate behemoths, Olivetti's own closely held family company, Ing. C. Olivetti & C., S. p. A., does not bulk large with its assets of some $100 million and its 24,000 or more employees; yet it is one of Italy's few massive industrial empires. Moreover in Italy, a country still hobbled by the habits of the past, still politically immature, still economically underdeveloped, what the Olivetti company does has an influence on the national scene far greater than a comparable American firm might wield on these shores. In this very different environment, Adriano Olivetti stands out as a major experimenter committed to the

Audit 302

An Olivetti panorama includes: (above, left to right) façade of the Chicago store; cover design for a folder; building at the machine tool division near Ivrea; outstanding typewriter designs, the LEXIKON 80 *above, the* LETTERA 22 *below; monument to founder Camillo Olivetti with background of waterfall; cover design. Below, left to right: entrance to Pozzuoli factory; adding and listing machine; cover design for calculator folder; Ivrea factory roof at night; company billboard designed by Pintori; cover design; passerby trying out typewriter mounted outside the New York store.*

most advanced developments of contemporary thought and technique. Yet he has come to stand out as well even in America. And this can be due only to the high originality of his style, which suffuses everything he touches.

Now fifty-eight, Olivetti heads a company that is just seven years younger than himself. It was founded by his father, Camillo, whose patriarchal image still presides over the far-flung works in a thousand votive photographs. In the company's parent town of Ivrea in northern Italy, Camillo's stern visage and flowing white beard are captured in an unusual metal sculpture by Emilio Greco which stands before a backdrop of cascading water. In the main factory itself there is an eerily lifelike mosaic statue of the old man that does full justice to his expansive *embonpoint,* once so characteristic of captains of industry.

Though the son's operations are now world-wide, Adriano's career is as deeply rooted as his father's in the Canavese Valley, that thin strip of hills and fields which leads to the Alps beyond. Ivrea, the capital of the region, is an hour by car from Milan to the east and half the time from Turin to the south. Around the town is a farming area broken up into unprosperous small holdings. Situated so near France and Switzerland, the region has been open to those winds of doctrine that have swept down from the north, leaving behind, among other things, islands of Protestantism and a strong

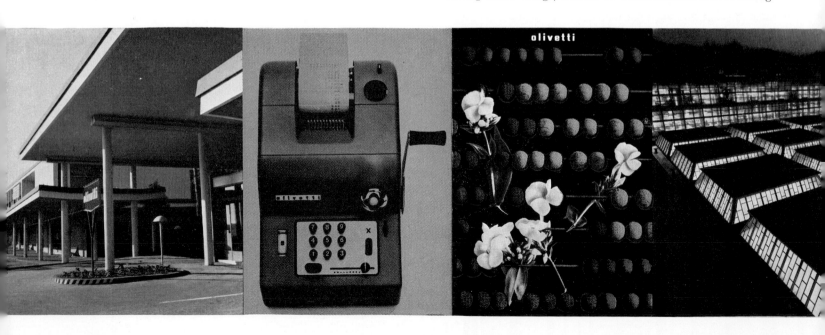

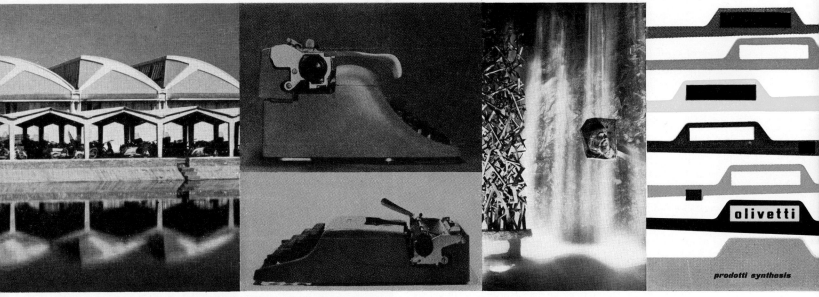

consciousness of the democratic process. It was here that Camillo Olivetti established his company and it is here that his son has tried to put his social theories into practice.

Camillo was the son of a well-to-do Jewish farmer and real-estate broker of the Canavese, and he married the daughter of a Waldensian pastor. Looking back at the moral atmosphere which surrounded this marriage, his son recently remarked: "Both my parents were strict and unbending. With my father a Jew and my mother a Protestant in Catholic Italy, they had that rigid moral code and devotion to work that persecuted people usually have. I remember one of the early books my father gave to me to read. It was an English book called *Self-Help*—a series of stories about memorable men of British history who had won their greatest victories in life by following the most moral of precepts. It was just like him."

Trained as an electrical engineer at the Turin Polytechnic, Camillo began his career at a moment when there was still a winning freshness about man's technological adventure. A year after his graduation in 1891 he went off to America as the companion of his former teacher Galileo Ferraris, who had just become famous as the discoverer of the magnetic field. With this trip began the close relationship between the Olivettis and the United States which still persists. Camillo met Edison and Steinmetz, was deeply impressed by American

machines, and spent two years teaching at Stanford University. Thirty-three years later, his son in turn visited America and assimilated its latest developments: industrial efficiency, the growth of a new managerial class, the power of advertising, and the necessity for social services.

While in the United States, Camillo had been struck by the notion of manufacturing typewriters; and this he set out to do soon after his return, although the project seemed somewhat quixotic in a country where the quill pen still flourished and good calligraphy was more precious than mechanical skill. Unwilling to copy any existing machine (although he later admitted that some were both cheaper to make and more efficient than his), the fledgling industrialist began from scratch, teaching his workmen the very rudiments of their new trade as he went along. The result was the famous M1, the first successful typewriter in Italy and the cornerstone of the Olivetti fortune.

All of Camillo's virtues are summed up in that first typewriter he designed. The M1 had a massive rectitude about it, as did Camillo himself. Although it was not a thing of beauty, it admirably suited his philosophy: "A typewriter should not be a gewgaw for the drawing room, ornate and in questionable taste. It should have an appearance that is serious and elegant at the same time."

Seriousness and elegance—these are key words in the

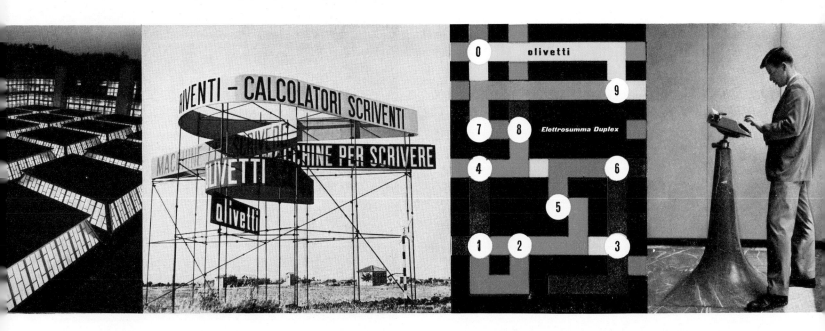

canon of both father and son. When Adriano grew up amid such precepts, his first thought as a student at Turin was to turn to journalism and political economy. Yet at the same time, "I felt that I should go into the family business . . . and when Fascism came to Italy there was nothing else I wanted to do." When he did enter the business, it was with a passionate interest in problems of design. To be sure, there were good practical reasons for such an interest. As Riccardo Musatti, a former art historian who now heads the firm's advertising and press department, has explained frankly, "Since Olivetti was behind in the office machine industry, it had to create the impression that it was ahead by resorting to the most modern presentation." But this still does not explain the intimate concern with which Adriano has followed and guided the work of the artists he has employed. It seems, rather, that he wanted to confer on the mass-produced products of the factory system a quality which would elevate them to something more than mere commodities. Beauty, after all, is a moral notion, and Olivetti is a moralist at heart.

In the late twenties, the Olivetti company reflected the state of Italian industrial design, which had got off to a lively start and then fallen back into eclectic, perfunctory, and sentimental habits. But by 1930 the philosophy of the Weimar Bauhaus group began to filter into Italy, just at the time when its influence in Germany was being undermined by the Nazis. The philosophy of this school was congenial to Olivetti's temper. It combined high technical skill with the purest aesthetic ideas. Besides, as one of his assistants has put it, "Olivetti's force is that he has always wanted to be in the vanguard." The Weimar school brought together workers in all the arts: the architects Mies Van der Rohe and Gropius; the painters Klee and Kandinsky; designers such as Herbert Bayer and Moholy-Nagy. In the early thirties, the painter Xanty Schawinsky, who had spent four fruitful years at the Bauhaus, came to work for Olivetti. Soon one could sense the direction the new Olivetti style was taking. The stern austerity of the Bauhaus was somewhat softened and made more poetic by the Italian atmosphere, but here was the same formidable use of photography, the brilliant play of type, and the disdain for irrelevant frippery which marked the Bauhaus style. By 1938, Olivetti had recruited an extraordinary team of designers who were to transform his wishes into reality in a series of startling posters, striking exhibition displays, and subtly conceived booklets. Among them was Leonardo Sinisgalli, a poet-engineer, and two young graduates from the art school at Monza, Constantino Nivola and Giovanni Pintori. Sinisgalli left the firm in 1940 and Nivola migrated to the United States, where his monumental sand sculpture was to preside over the Olivetti Fifth Avenue showroom years later. But Pintori remained, and to this day he is one of the master designers who shape the Olivetti company's public image.

Discussing the role Olivetti himself played in creating the company style, Pintori recently remarked: "At the begin-

ning, he was intimately involved with everything we did. He not only chose the men who did the work, but he gave suggestions and criticisms of the finished work down to the last detail. Particularly with architects, he was constantly involved in the job—but with us too. He is a man teeming with intuition. He has a style and although he may not be able to fabricate it in any special way he knows how to communicate its sense and then to judge its results."

Musatti put it this way: "Olivetti has always insisted that we must present the ideal of a mechanical culture, that we must give the idea that the machine, the typewriter, is the last word in modern culture. Do you remember one of Pintori's most famous posters? On the left was an inkwell with an old-fashioned pen. In the inkwell was a beautiful rose. To the right there was nothing but the words Olivetti Studio 42. The pen belongs to the romantic past; the typewriter is of the world of today."

Olivetti's concern is with the present and the future. As Musatti says: "History does not interest him unless it bears directly on what he is doing. He never enjoys it for itself. He likes books which contain the most contemporary thought. In fact, his publishing house specializes in such volumes. He is not a collector of old paintings, nor does he like old people. You know, we put out those lovely calendars with their reproductions of Raphael, Piero della Francesca, and Etruscan paintings. Olivetti is really not very interested in them. He lets us do it because he knows that they are good and bring good will, but he is really not enthusiastic. . . . He is a rare Italian, not only because he has few intimates, but because he is ready to renounce tradition."

He has even renounced some traditions of modern industrial specialization, believing that a man of intelligence and feeling can be equally successful in different jobs. The artist Marcello Nizzoli, for example, was first hired by Olivetti to execute designs illustrating publicity slogans. When he first arrived on the scene in 1931, however, Olivetti was in the process of working out new body casings for his office machines which would set them off from the others on the market. Nizzoli was drawn into the project and helped to design the SUMMA calculating machine. This experience led to his great triumph of 1948, the body design of the standard typewriter LEXIKON 80, widely regarded as one of the most elegant products of the industrial age—a machine that stands solid and graceful like some sculpture Brancusi might have made. It was followed by another Nizzoli success, the portable LETTERA 22, whose efficient charm has made it a favorite among international newspaper correspondents in particular. (Recently, however, the introduction of a series of deplorable pastel tones as alternatives to the soft greyish-beige which has long distinguished the Olivetti machines has come as a shock to their many admirers—including correspondents.)

Of all the arts, the one which engages Olivetti most is architecture (together with its corollary, city planning), for it is here that his aesthetic and social preoccupations meet

This colorful fantasy of numbers is a cover design by Giovanni Pintori for a booklet on the company's Printing Calculator.

in a very concrete manner. *Il Ingegnere,* as he is known to his colleagues, has always lavished his closest attention on the buildings which house the Olivetti enterprise, from the celebrated complex of modern structures which has grown up in and around Ivrea since 1934 to his glamourous showrooms in far-off countries. When a new addition to the Olivetti landscape is planned, Adriano can turn to the brilliant stable of architects who have worked with him for so many years (Luigi Figini, Gino Pollini, and Ernesto Rogers, to mention only three). But he is just as likely to commission someone new, off the beaten track—as he did when he asked Luigi Cosenza to design the most recent Olivetti factory (1952–1955) in Pozzuoli, a few miles west of Naples.

Luigi Cosenza is an Italian engineer with left-wing sympathies, and the former owner of a bouncing lion cub which he kept as a pet. To him the memory of his association with the capitalist Olivetti is an unalloyed pleasure. "You meet one friend like Olivetti," he said when I saw him recently in Naples, "and it's possible; otherwise, it's impossible. He is not a man who is always saying No, do it like this. He respects other men."

Cosenza's gusts of talk filled the old-fashioned, cavernous room in the antiquated apartment house looking out over the Bay of Naples. A huge photograph of Lenin's head presided over the conversation. Cosenza told how excited he had been when he heard that Olivetti planned to build a factory near Naples. He wryly remembered how excited a hundred other architects and engineers in Italy had been at the news, for they besieged *Il Ingegnere* when he visited Sorrento for a rest. Cosenza waited a few days and then wrote to Olivetti, asking if he could pay a visit. Agreed. When he arrived Olivetti said to him, "Come, let's eat a good fish in peace." Afterwards Cosenza pulled out a sheaf of small sketches he had made which embodied his ideas for the new plant. Olivetti was reserved and cautious.

Cosenza's visit evoked bitter complaints from those who thought it was outrageous to give such work to a leftist. The comments annoyed Olivetti, who likes his freedom. Soon after, the architect was invited to Rome where discussions were continued. "Without Olivetti's support the factory could never have been built," insisted Cosenza. "All the Olivetti technicians objected to my plan. They didn't like my idea of a main building in the shape of a great cross. They were afraid they couldn't tamper with it.

"But I got the job. It was my first factory. Yes, I would have liked to do a factory anywhere. But I particularly liked the idea of Pozzuoli. I preferred it to Naples. Olivetti himself tried to avoid Naples. He wanted Pozzuoli to have the same relation to Naples as Ivrea does to Milan. That is, outside of the city, a pilot experiment for a depressed area.

"I shared his view. Moreover, I wanted to make the factory less like a prison. You can't change the fact that it is a prison, but I wanted to make it as different from the old-fashioned factory as I could. I know that Olivetti feels the

same way. We are good friends in cultural matters and good enemies in politics.

"They said you couldn't call a building like that a factory, but it worked. The place is not only beautiful, but profitable. Productivity is as good here as it is in the north, despite what they said about the bad habits of workmen of the south and the design of the building."

In Italy, the Pozzuoli plant occupies a unique place. It is an emissary from the north to the south, from one Italy to another, from the thriving, industrial area of Piedmont to the hard-pressed, underdeveloped regions that begin below Rome and go all the way down to the tip of the Italian boot.

Like many thoughtful Italians, Olivetti feels that Italy will remain an underdeveloped country unless the problem of the south is solved. Unlike most Italians he was in a position to do something about it. He chose Pozzuoli as the site for this experiment: a poor town with little employment, yet not so poor as to be crushed. His aim was to found a productive enterprise in the presumably inefficient south, and to lure other industry to the area if it were successful.

The factory which Luigi Cosenza built for Olivetti at Pozzuoli is something different indeed. Until one steps through the gleaming glass front doors and marches through the bare lobby, flanked by elevators, there is little to suggest that it is a factory at all.

From the Via Domitiana, which passes the main façade, the building might be taken for an elegant resort hotel or a sanatorium in the modern style. For there in the background are the heights of Mount Campiglione, and stretching before the factory is the Gulf of Baia, with Capri and Ischia visible in the distance when the day is clear. Cosenza has created a plant which is unique in its sense of freedom and elegance. From every bench and point on the assembly line there is a view of the outdoors. Light pours in with all its Mediterranean clarity and abundance. Spotted here and there among the low buildings which are joined together in a coherent whole are ponds caught in free-form concrete walls. Landscaping encloses the entire industrial bulk and reunites it with nature.

As in every Olivetti establishment, the social service facilities seem to take precedence over everything else. Leading from the factory itself, through a large airy locker room next to the dining hall, is the Olivetti version of the welfare state: a clinic equipped as well as the best Italian hospital, a library filled with such unlikely authors as Faulkner, Gide, Bennett, and Shaw, and an elaborate recreation hall. All are elegant, clean, and obviously well used. Nearby are the apartment houses he has built for his workers. So splendid is the whole establishment that there is a wry truth to the remark which the director of the plant made as he summed up the effect of the factory on the people of Pozzuoli: "For those who haven't found employment here, the factory is like Kafka's castle. It is a kind of Paradise where the lucky ones have gained entrance."

The Olivetti social services go far beyond what the Italian state does for its citizens. They touch upon every aspect of a worker's life—in some cases from the moment he is conceived until the day he dies. A woman employee who becomes pregnant is granted a paid leave beginning three months before her child is born and continuing for six months afterward. During all this time she receives more comfort and better medical care than most women in Italy. For a trivial sum her child may then attend a superbly designed and competently staffed factory nursery during the next six years until he is ready for school. As he grows older he can go to the mountains or the seaside for a twenty-five-day camp vacation at the company's expense. And then, at fifteen, if a boy has talent he can begin a complete technical education, paid for by the Olivetti firm, which can lead even to a university education for the very brightest, also paid for by the company. For the rest, the fringe benefits which the Olivetti worker enjoys include spotless clinics, libraries, cultural programs, low-priced company housing, and low-interest loans to buy an automobile or a motor scooter, cheap meals, and a wage better than the nationally negotiated standard. Indeed it sometimes seems that the whole Olivetti enterprise exists for these social services, although its own profits belie this. Some services were instituted as long ago as 1909, but only since Adriano assumed control of the company have they become central to the over-all Olivetti scheme. For him, they are a way of changing the world, perhaps dearer to his heart than the business of manufacturing office equipment which he does with such great success.

Except for cries of "paternalism" from the left, there seems to be little debate about the merits of the Olivetti social services. But his social and political ideas have carried him far beyond his own factories, into the field of community planning and, then, into the more debatable role of social prophet. As of 1959 he is the founder and head of a political party with a vast program of social reform and one representative—himself—in the national assembly, a seat which cost him a small fortune and a great effort to win. This was a dubious victory for a man who by his own admission "has no taste for parliamentary life."

I went to see Olivetti at his Roman offices, in a converted *palazzo* a few paces from the Spanish Steps, where he has done much of his work since his election to public office. It is evident that he does not feel as much at home here as he does in the shiny new office building that serves as his company's headquarters in Milan, from which he can walk past La Scala to visit his publishing house, or cross the great cathedral square to the design studio that produces the posters and booklets which carry the Olivetti name around the world. And neither appeals to him as much as his rambling, old-fashioned house perched on a hill of Ivrea, overlooking his ancestral domain. Compared to his haunts in the Italian north, his Roman offices seem transient, lavish as they are. Expanses of white marble and mirrored woodwork set off

CONTINUED ON PAGE 127

A CHANGE FOR ITALIAN CHILDREN

For the children of Olivetti employees the company provides free summer holiday camps such as the one above, on the Tyrrhenian Sea, near the main Ivrea plant. In southern Italy, where the company has a new factory at Pozzuoli, these modern Olivetti camps offer a striking contrast to the nearby streets of Naples (below).

The ballerina photographed in three roles: made-up as the sinister Insect

Allegra Kent

Talent, ambition, and the masterly touch of Balanchine have gone into the making of a sparkling new ballerina

Queen for The Cage *and in a movement of attack from that ballet; in a joyous arabesque from* Pastorale; *and* sur les pointes *in* Swan Lake.

Among the spectators who saw the Bolshoi Ballet at the Metropolitan Opera House last spring, none watched the soaring Russian dancers with keener personal interest than a young lady of twenty-two who sat (and sometimes stood) through most of their New York performances. She found the ballerinas "marvelous, perfect," but thought their dancing "old-fashioned, of another style, a long-ago style." She envied their lives: "So different from ours . . . so cared for. They don't have to worry about food or clothing or making ends meet. They

have a place in the country where they can all go for weekends and holidays. They can think only of their work." And something else she envied Soviet ballerinas: "The men, such heroic types, so virile. In ballet it is right for women to dance with men. Each sex emphasizes the qualities of the other. It gives you a wonderful feeling to be lifted, carried, held."

From these comments it would not be hard to deduce that the young lady is herself an American ballerina, that she has lived the lean, hamburgers-and-milk-shakes life of a dancer in New York be-

tween seasons, and that she is trained in the modern style identified with George Balanchine. Allegra Kent is, in fact, the brightest young star of American ballet and the prize pupil, not to say creation, of Mr. Balanchine.

In an era when little girls are popped into ballet class almost as automatically as their brothers are enrolled in the Little League, Miss Kent is every eager young ballerina's dream come true. She spent her childhood in California where she attended the Ojai Valley School. "When I was nine," she remembers, "I used to watch the boys swinging on vines across the brook. I envied them, being able to fly so lightly. I thought then that I must dance." She studied with Carmelita Maracci and Madame Nijinska. When she was fourteen her mother took her to New York and presented her at Balanchine's School of American Ballet. "My mother is a very determined woman," Miss Kent reflects. "She told Mr. Balanchine that I should have a scholarship, and he agreed."

In the next year she led the double life of high school student in the morning and ballet student in the afternoon. "I would finish school at 2:15," she recalls, "and go dashing down the street with my blouse unbuttoned, practically out of my clothes, to make ballet class at 2:30." A year later, at fifteen, she became a member of the New York City Ballet's *corps.*

If Allegra Kent's success is due in the first instance to a great natural talent and intensive effort, it owes no less to the rigorous, inspired training of her teacher. George Balanchine is the living titan of twentieth-century choreographers. As artistic director of the New York City Ballet, he has created the most adventurous dance company in the world. Although he was himself trained in the Imperial School of Russia (and was there a classmate of the Bolshoi's incomparable Galina Ulanova) and was Diaghilev's last choreographer, Balanchine has not been content with preserving the classics of nineteenth- and early twentieth-century ballet as they were conceived in Russia and are still performed there by the magnificent but archaic Bolshoi. *Swan Lake*—and at that, only the second of its four acts—is one of the two classics performed by the New York City Ballet. With the genius of the true creator, Balanchine has chosen to pursue the most advanced ideas of dance in concert with Igor Stravinsky and other musical explorers. To the atonal, serial music of such composers, Balanchine has moved ever toward more abstract, unprogrammatic dance. Seldom do panting princes pursue elusive dryads in his works, but boys and girls in stark leotards move with labyrinthine gestures to music more suggestive of analytical geometry than romance.

To create his own style of dance, Balanchine has had to train his own kind of dancer. Among his ballerinas have been Vera Zorina, Maria Tallchief, and Tanaquil LeClerq, all of whom bear his unmistakable stamp and all of whom, incidentally, he married. But no one dancing today is quite so much his own creation as Allegra Kent. She alone has developed entirely within the ranks of the company.

Save for the alluring name she has had since birth, Allegra Kent off stage has about as much glamour as any pony-tailed college sophomore on a weekday. On stage she is a creature of arresting beauty with a superbly lithe and expressive body. She is blessed with remarkable arms and wrists as well as splendid ankles and insteps. With these feet and the straight knees that favor a ballerina, she exhibits in her best work a characteristically tense and snappy step, driven from the heel, that rivets the eye. Gleaming in white body make-up, she moves with pristine grace and elegance.

In a profession not unknown for professional jealousies, Miss Kent has enjoyed the friendship and help of the older principal ballerinas in the company. She readily acknowledges that her model has been Maria Tallchief, whose style has the icy glitter of a flame caught in a web of crystal. Melissa Hayden has helped her, not only in her approach to a role, but in such refinements as the tricks of make-up. Diana Adams has been both mentor and confidant, providing the quiet counsel and, knowingly or not, the moral arm on which the younger ballerina could lean.

It was during the company's tour of Australia in 1958, according to her own estimation, that Miss Kent came into her own as a ballerina. "It was a horrible trip," she recalls. "And the Australians didn't like us a bit. All of us hated it. The ballerinas were glad to let others dance roles they had always guarded for themselves. Before we left, Balanchine had a *Swan Lake* costume made for me and it was packed without my knowing it." He was not on the tour but Diana Adams taught her the role of the Swan Queen. "The whole thing wore me down," Miss Kent remembers, "trying to learn so much so soon, *Swan Lake* and other roles. But it did stretch my talent continuously."

Miss Kent has been through quite a stretching process. After accepting her in his school, Balanchine soon tried her mettle, and, acting as a sort of aesthetic chiropractor, singled her out for special attention. "He drove me constantly, forcing me to develop," she says. For the past seven years she has lived on a demanding regimen. It has not always been easy to reconcile the process of maturing as an

PHOTOGRAPHS BY ELLIOTT ERWITT

Her splendid line, perhaps the most distinguishing feature of a ballerina, is captured in this photograph of Allegra Kent by Elliott Erwitt. She displays it while dancing Apollo, *the first acknowledged masterpiece choreographed by George Balanchine. This movement is formally termed* grand jeté.

artist to that of being a young girl. And if Miss Kent is not precisely the girl down the block, she has all her inclinations, from collecting sea shells, to picnicking in Central Park, to having a try at romance. At one point, deciding that she was inadequately educated, she abruptly withdrew from the company and entered college—or two of them in quick succession—but after a few months and an attack of acute nostalgia she was back at the *barre* under Balanchine's scrutiny.

Miss Kent was elevated to the rank of ballerina at eighteen. Because Balanchine has chosen to discourage the concept of prima ballerina, she shares top billing with five other principal dancers. This season she will be seen as the principal soloist in twenty-two leading roles.

Without doubt her triumph has been in *The Seven Deadly Sins,* that fusion of dance, opera, and drama that Balanchine choreographed in 1933 for the premiere of the Kurt Weill-Berthold Brecht fable. As the maiden who leaves the family home in Louisiana with an alter-ego older sister (commandingly played by Lotte Lenya, the composer's widow, who herself seems a Max Beckmann painting out of the awful German disillusion which gave rise to this work), and sets out to support the Bible-backed old folks at home, Miss Kent is immensely touching.

The role of Anna II is perfectly suited to Miss Kent in several ways, not the least of which is physical. Her young girl's body conveys an air of fragility not displayed by the other ballerinas of this company. There is an open-eyed freshness about her, with the hint of deep stirrings beneath, which lends her a presence, a radiance in the role, that is apart from her conscious contribution to it.

If she does not cherish this role as an index of her mastery as a dancer, it could be because little pure dance is called for as she delineates the pathetic but fascinating creature: a girl forced by circumstances to pander to men who wallow with her in The Seven Deadly Sins before she is thrown up, used and yet oddly clean, like blanched driftwood on the shore of life. The role is theatrical and in this fact may lie a clue to the future of

Miss Kent. With every sinew of her body she conveys emotions precisely as an actress.

One more note about Allegra Kent as Anna II: For some period in this ballet she is required to disport herself clad only in black lace panties and bra, barefoot, and with long hair down. Despite her girlish frame Allegra Kent is the sexiest-looking ballerina in history.

To turn the coin, her *Swan Lake,* so far, has held a measure of disappointment. Fresh from seeing Maya Plisetskaya of the Bolshoi assault the role of Odette-Odile, Queen of the Swans, with such passion and virtuosity as to paralyze the observer, some viewers were not greatly moved by Miss Kent's technically fine but relatively placid performance. Though in this role Miss Kent is served by her physique and the great beauty of line it affords her, that body does not throb with emotion, or project it adequately in the elegiac passages.

The role of the Swan Queen is one of those few classics by which stars are internationally judged. By now all the possibilities of the role have been seen, or at least sensed, in the performances of such prima ballerinas as Pavlova, Markova, Fonteyn. Some of them took years to develop their mastery of the role (Plisetskaya is thirty-five years old). Miss Kent is lovely to look at as the ephemeral Odette, and gives pleasure if less than complete satisfaction. It should be remembered that she learned the role only last year.

In *The Cage* Miss Kent is obliged to personify a female insect destroying the male in a macabre orgy that is one of the triumphs of the choreographer Jerome Robbins. Few insects from a coleopterist's shadow box are so handsome as Miss Kent, but it may be supposed that she does not understand or relish this aspect of feminine destructiveness. The part requires a generation of malice that is not forthcoming, although Miss Kent dances the role with style and skill.

In some of those febrile and startling inventions by which Balanchine demonstrates his supreme musical surety, Miss Kent is particularly satisfying. His mas-

terpiece *Agon,* set to the Stravinsky score, is such a work; so is *Episodes*—which he and Martha Graham jointly choreographed, in separate parts—to the music of Anton von Webern. To this dense, repetitively discordant music, moving with its furious tempi, Mr. Balanchine has designed dense, rapidly articulated movements at a pace and style that would dismay the most accomplished dancers in many leading companies of the world. Frequently he arranges his figures as unfolding, fluttering notes and phrases on the musical scale. Dancers are required to move with dazzling brilliance *in situ,* conveying an extraordinary sense of vertical and centripetal movement, rather than the grand, lateral motion with which most audiences are familiar from conventional ballets. Frequently they seem to be so many pinwheels governed by some Rube Goldberg motor. Mr. Balanchine has trained his dancers to come along with him on these hegiras to new frontiers of dance, even though some accompany him reluctantly, hankering after the showy, individual posturing of the classic roles. Miss Kent seems now to have been bred to voyage on these adventures, and she operates as precisely as if a metronome had been implanted in her bosom by Maestro Stravinsky himself.

Altogether there is no doubt that Miss Kent is a ballerina of delicious range. She performs with aplomb and a certain largeness in *Apollo,* Balanchine's first masterwork, created for Diaghilev to the score by Stravinsky; she is an enchanting nymph in Jerome Robbins's vision of *Afternoon of a Faun* set to the Debussy score; and she turns out to be a fetching hoyden of the dance halls in Balanchine's *Western Symphony,* by Hershy Kay.

Even among ballerinas Miss Kent's rise has been meteoric. What remains for her to achieve is that absolute reign on the stage, that easy domination of the audience, that total projection which is attained only by the greatest artists when the heart of the matter is fully comprehended and exploited. Meanwhile she has that priceless key to greatness, total dedication to her art. And she is twenty-two.

—R.E.G

By H. R. TREVOR-ROPER

It was not the medieval world
that produced the witchcraft delusion.
It was the age of the Renaissance
and the Enlightenment. An English
historian examines the forces that nurtured it
and the forces that finally overcame it.

THE PERSECUTION OF WITCHES

Three witches are burned, and two confederates executed, in Germany in 1555

The Dark Ages were not all that dark. They were sensible about witches. To believe in witches or werewolves, said Saint Boniface in the eighth century, was unchristian. In the tenth century a Church dignitary declared night-flying a hallucination, and his declaration was accepted into the canon law. In the eleventh, the laws of King Coloman of Hungary refused to notice witches "since they do not exist." Of course, shepherds and peasant women continued to talk of them, as they had done in pagan times: we find sympathetic magic in Theocritus, werewolves in Petronius, anointment and night-flying in Apuleius; and Saint Augustine, with his African credulity, did his best to preserve these peasant superstitions and fit them into his gigantic system. But in general the Church, as the civilizer of nations, disdained such old wives' tales. They were the rubbish of paganism which the light of the Gospel had dispelled. Even the Devil, in the Middles Ages, sank through familiarity into contempt. The Prince of Darkness became a village hobgoblin, dismissible with a formula.

And then, with the end of the Middle Ages, what a change! In the sixteenth century, the century of the Renaissance, and the seventeenth century, the century of the

New Science, all Europe seemed given over to witches. Scotland and Hungary, where they had hitherto been unknown, were suddenly found to be swarming with them. By their own confession, thousands of old women every night anointed themselves with "devil's grease," slipped through cracks and keyholes and up chimneys, and flew off to the witches' Sabbath. There they worshiped the Devil in the form of a stinking goat, danced around him amid macabre music, kissed him solemnly under the tail. and feasted on such viands as tempted their national imagination. In Germany these

The Devil's converts (as shown in a tract of 1626) enter into a pact with him by stamping on the Cross.

were sliced turnips, parodies of the Host; in Spain, exhumed corpses, preferably of kinsfolk; in England, more sensibly, roast beef and beer. When not thus engaged, these old ladies, it seemed, were busy suckling familiar spirits in the form of weasels, moles, bats, toads, or other convenient creatures; they were compassing the death of their neighbors or their neighbors' pigs; they were raising tempests, causing blights, or procuring impotence in bridegrooms; and as a pledge of their servitude they were constantly having sexual intercourse with the Devil, who appeared (since even he abhors unnatural vice) to she-witches as an incubus, to he-witches as a succubus.

What Gibbon called "the chaste severity of the Fathers" was much exercised by this last subject, and no detail escaped their learned scrutiny. They established that as a lover the Devil was of "freezing coldness" to the touch, and certain items were lacking in his equipment; but there was no frigidity in the technical sense: his attentions were of formidable, even oppressive,

solidity. That he could generate on witches was agreed by nearly all (how else, asked the Catholic doctors, could the birth of Luther be explained?); but was that power the Devil's own, as a Franciscan specialist maintained ("under correction from our holy Mother Church"), or did he, being neuter, operate with borrowed matter? Some important theologians conjectured that the Devil equipped himself by squeezing the organs of the dead; others had other theories, more profound than decent; but on the whole holy Mother Church followed the magisterial ruling of the Angelic Doctor, Saint Thomas Aquinas. The Devil, she ruled, could only discharge as incubus what he had previously absorbed as succubus: he therefore nimbly alternated between these postures. It seems surprising that the Roman Church, which has never renounced these beliefs, should not have recalled them to prove the diabolical nature of artificial insemination donors.

What was the Church to do when faced with this alarming epidemic of witches? What indeed except discover, test, and destroy them? To discover them, village hatreds must be exploited, German schoolboys trained to denounce, confessors supplied with elaborate questionnaires. To test them, there were certain reliable evidences, or *indicia*. Unless one was lucky enough to discover "a pot full of human limbs, sacred things, hosts, etc.," which, as an inquisitor sagely observed, "is a grave *indicium*," one had to be content with circumstantial tests. Of these, fortunately, there were plenty: a mole or wart, by which the familiar spirit was suckled; an insensitive spot that did not bleed when pricked; a capacity to float in water; an incapacity to shed tears; or even the mere aspect of a witch—old, ugly, or smelly. And then there were certain professions that were automatically suspect. It was well known, for instance, that midwives were ordered by the Devil to destroy newborn infants. If anything went wrong at childbirth, that too must be a grave *indicium*.

When the witch was thus identified, the next thing was to make her confess. On the Continent, and in Scotland, this was easy. There were the torturer and the questionnaire. Witchcraft being *crimen exceptum*, there was no limit to the torture, and many and various were the instruments and re-

finements used. There were the *grésillons*, which crushed the tips of fingers and toes in a vice; the *échelle*, or rack, for stretching the body, the *tortillon* for squeezing its tender parts at the same time; and the *estrapade*, or pulley for jerking it violently in mid-air. All these were used liberally in Lorraine. In Scotland, the legs of the suspect were broken, even into fragments, in the boot, or grilled on the *caschielawis*; the thumb was screwed in the *pilliwinckes*; the fingernails were pulled off with the *turkas*, or pincers, and needles were driven up to their heads into the quick. Elsewhere the ingenuity of the torturers had contrived other exquisite devices. As for the questionnaire, that made confession simple: the learned details were ready to hand, and the victim had only to say yes. Hence the detailed identity of witches' confessions. If the witch did confess, her guilt was held to be proved and clerical science confirmed; but she was expected, of course, to name all those neighbors and kinsfolk whom she had seen at the Sabbath. Even without torture, there were many self-accusing exhibitionists who were only too glad to give this "special evidence." In this way whole villages were decimated, and even judges sometimes took fright at the ever-expanding complicity. If the suspect did not confess, her guilt and her torture were both increased. To be a witch and deny it, and deny it even under torture, was evidence of the blackest guilt: such courage, it was agreed, could only proceed from hardened wickedness and the help of the Devil. In either case, whether she confessed or not, the witch was sent to the flames—unless, as a special "grace" from the bishop or abbot or secular lord, she was merely torn with red-hot pincers and beheaded.

In England, it is fair to add, the methods were milder. There was no Holy Inquisition in England. Also there was no torture in English common law, only discomfort (though the distinction could sometimes be blurred). Moreover, in England condemned witches were hanged not burned. When Oliver Cromwell conquered Scotland and introduced English justice, persecution almost ceased, much to the indignation of the Presbyterian clergy. Nor was the doctrine so fully developed in England as on the Continent. The "witch-mark," the insensitive spot which revealed the witch—and which sometimes gathered four surgeons with long needles round a Continental suspect, pricking, till mere paralysis procured the necessary insensitivity—was not recognized in England.

How can such lunacy have possessed humanity for two centuries? It seems inconceivable, and yet, though the numbers have often been greatly exaggerated, the facts are not in doubt. Now, with the republication of the unfinished work of the great American historian H. C. Lea, we can trace the whole history of the craze and the persecution. It was his work on *The History of the Inquisition*—that monument of liberal scholarship—that led Lea, in his last years, to turn his mind to the closely related subject of witchcraft. Unfortunately, he died when he had merely collected the materials. But the materials alone, with his commentary, are a magnificent historical work. Arranged and published half a century after the author's death, they enable us better than any other work to trace the causes and history of the European witch mania: a history of collective cruelty and credulity instituted, inflamed, and prolonged (though not always controlled) by organized religion.

For there can be no doubt that the witch craze was organized, and received its final organization late in the fifteenth century, by the medieval Church. Little by little, in the later Middle Ages, the Church had equated witchcraft with the more serious crimes of sorcery and heresy, and the Schoolmen had systematized, embellished, and condemned those hitherto disregarded superstitions and hallucinations that spring, at bottom, from rural poverty. By such attentions they had built up and advertised a grotesque new mythology for which the inquisitors afterwards, by their torture and their questionnaires, obtained massive confirmation.

For it is quite clear that witchcraft, as a systematic cult, was not discovered; it was invented by the inquisitors. We can trace the movement in all its stages by dates and places. Everywhere it is the same: first the persecutors, then the heresy. It was the inquisitors who discovered the first witches in Hungary and Scotland and who spread the epidemic over Germany. Elsewhere half the details to which thousands of witches readily and unanimously confessed had been quite unknown in their districts until the inquisitors had arrived with their books and pincers. And the crucial date can be pinpointed. In 1484 the Dominican inquisitors in the bigoted Alpine valleys, where they had long been burning witches, sought to increase their power, extend their field, and silence their critics by calling in papal help. So they solicited from Pope Innocent VIII the first general Witch-Bull, the Bull *Summis Desiderantes Affectibus*. Two years later the same inquisitors, as if in response to the Bull, advertised the disease they were now armed and authorized to cure. They published the first great encyclopedia of the subject, *Malleus Maleficarum*, the Hammer of Witches. From that date the delusion began its fabulous course. From the Swiss valleys papal authority sent it out over all Europe. The disease was created by its pretended remedy.

At first the educated laity were contemptuous of this clerical nonsense. How could lawyers, scholars, philosophers, in the age of Erasmus, swallow these Alpine credulities, this monkish phantasmagoria? The

In homage to their new master, the initiates offer the Devil black candles and kneel to kiss his buttocks.

European humanists, putting (as the clergy sourly complained) human reason before divine theology, poured eloquent scorn on yet another instance of barbarous folly. Witchcraft, said the great Italian scientist Girolamo Cardano, in 1550, was merely an illusion of minds distorted by poverty and undernourishment, and confessions were therefore worthless. But against massive, systematic propaganda who can hold out? Clerical machinery was organized; lay intelligence was not. Moreover, the clergy controlled education. So, as encyclopedia followed encyclopedia, as commentator quoted commentator, as confession echoed confession, the sheer weight of documented rubbish ultimately overwhelmed even the most rational mind. In Catholic countries the clergy, having survived the Protestant threat, redoubled their control over all departments of life. The result was the *sacrificio dell' intelletto,* the sacrifice of the intellect: a sacrifice made easier by that other phenomenon, which we also know, *la trahison des clercs,* the treason of the intellectuals.

Such was the Catholic Counter Reformation. Nor did the Protestant Reformation help—as yet. Luther was as credulous as any Schoolman; and the Swiss Reformers, in addition, breathed the same Alpine bigotry as the Catholic inquisitors. Indeed, it was in consequence of their resort to Geneva and Basle and other purified "schools of Christ" that the Marian exiles carried the craze back to Elizabethan England, to Calvinist Scotland, and to New England. Besides, there was that phrase in the Bible, their Bible: "thou shalt not suffer a witch to live." "The Bible," said Calvin firmly, preaching to the Elect about the Witch of Endor, "teaches that there are witches and that they must be slain. . . . God expressly commands that all witches and enchantresses shall be put to death; and this law of God is an universal law."

So in Geneva, which before had been free from witch trials, Calvin introduced a new reign of terror: in the sixty years after his coming, one hundred and fifty witches were burned. Moreover, in Protestant as in Catholic lands, the rules of evidence were now quietly changed. There was to be no nonsense about proof of material damage: to *be* a witch, even a harmless witch, was enough. In Calvinist Scotland, in the Lutheran and then Calvinist Palatinate, in Lutheran Saxony, the law was adjusted accordingly. Witches must be destroyed, declared the Elector of Saxony, "even if their sorcery has harmed nobody." In England the law preserved the old distinction, and the Anglican Church preserved an honorable record of sanity and moderation; but if the Calvinist clergy had had their way, it would have been changed. "Death," declared the oracle of Cambridge Puritanism William Perkins, "is the just and deserved punishment" even "of the good witch." And

Perkins, who also advocated the introduction of torture into England for such cases, was "our Perkins," the revered teacher of the Founding Fathers of New England.

Thus, as the sixteenth century went on, all Europe, Catholic and Protestant alike, was infected. The clergy vied with each other in ferocious absurdity, the lawyers followed obediently in their wake, and the laws were duly tightened up. Even the intellectuals surrendered. By 1580 Jean Bodin, one of the greatest of French thinkers, had joined the hue and cry. Himself a judge and burner of witches, he attacked his king as their defender, argued that judges who spared them should themselves be executed, and approved anonymous denunciation and lynch law. In Lorraine Nicolas Rémy, *procureur-général* of the duchy, a cultivated scholar, historian, and poet, sent two or three thousand victims to the stake and even so thought the laws too mild. By law, children who were said to have attended their mother at the Sabbath were merely flogged in front of the fire in which their mother was burning; Rémy would have had the whole seed of witches exterminated, and he pointed (to show that Catholics too could quote the Old Testament) to the irreverent children whom Elisha so properly caused to be devoured by bears. In Germany, in the next century, Benedict Carpzov was regarded as the greatest jurist of his time. He was a devout Lutheran and his handbook on witches was honored as the *Malleus* of Protestantism. Reflecting on his meritorious career, he boasted that he had read the Bible from cover to cover fifty-three times, taken the Holy Sacrament every week, greatly intensified the efficacy of torture, and procured the death of twenty thousand witches. In England the most liberal of judges, Sir Matthew Hale, an enlightened natural scientist and humane reformer of the law, hanged an old woman on the evidence of a wart; Joseph Glanvill, a Baconian scientist and Fellow of the Royal Society, devoted his intellectual energy to the confutation of the Sadducees who disbelieved in witches; and the Cambridge Platonist and rational theologian Henry More was perfectly ready to believe not only that his own urine smelt of violets but also that an old man had sailed over Shelford steeple by night and torn his breeches on the weathercock.

No doubt there were skeptics, too; but who would dare to express skepticism where the churches had power and the lawyers, as usual, conformed? "It is rating our conjectures high," wrote the discreet Montaigne, after witnessing the trial and confession of a batch of witches at the court of some petty prince, "to roast other people alive for them"; but even that discretion was silenced as Montaigne joined all other

The witches are now prepared to practice their evil powers. Houses, at their whim, are consumed by flames.

critics of the witch mania on the Roman Index. Others, as they were more explicit, suffered more directly. In 1589 Dietrich Flade, rector of the university and chief judge of the electoral court at Trier, found himself unconvinced by the confessions, under torture, of the old women who were brought before him. He therefore judged them with leniency. At once the Prince-Archbishop had him arrested, accused of witchcraft, tortured till he confessed whatever was put to him, strangled, and burnt.

A generation later the German Jesuit Friedrich von Spee was converted by his own experiences as a confessor of condemned witches. "Torture," he declared roundly in 1631, "fills our Germany with witches and unheard-of wickedness, and not only Germany but any nation that tries it. . . . If all of us have not confessed ourselves witches, that is only because we have not all been tortured." And who, he asked, were the men who demanded these tortures? Jurists in search of gain, credulous villagers, and "those theologians and prelates who quietly enjoy their speculations and know nothing of the squalor of prisons, the weight of chains, the implements of torture, the lamentations of the poor—things

far beneath their dignity."

Spee's book, *Cautio Criminalis*, is one of the most eloquent protests against the witch craze in Germany: it has earned him more lasting fame than his poetry and caused him to be called "saint and martyr by a higher canonization than that of the Church." But what fury it caused in his Order! For in many places the Jesuits, as the paladins of orthodoxy, led the hunt. To escape the wrath of his colleagues, Spee's book was published anonymously, without the knowledge of his superiors, in the relative freedom of a Protestant city.

Even in England, in the days of Puritan influence, one had to be careful. Under Queen Elizabeth, Reginald Scot, a country gentleman, boldly attacked the belief in witches. At once the king of Scotland rushed to its defense. He was a firm believer and fancied himself as a demonologist—indeed, he claimed to have been personally inconvenienced by a storm at sea raised by the co-operation of Scottish and Norwegian witches. Naturally he was enraged by Scot's skepticism. Moreover, since he was heir to the English throne, his rage could be disagreeable. Twenty years later, when he came into his new kingdom, his adversary was safely dead, but the impious book was seized and burned by the hangman. After that, although "the frequency of forged possessions" converted King James himself to sense, his less privileged subjects took no risks. Even Sir Francis Bacon and John Selden, two of the greatest lay minds in England, were careful to frame their undoubted skepticism in discreet, orthodox terms.

Meanwhile, the persecution abroad went on. Torture, of course, was the basis of it. "Now my dearest child," a burgomaster of Bamberg wrote to his daughter in 1628, after having publicly confessed that he had renounced God, given himself to the Devil, and met his fellow officials of Bamberg at a witches' Sabbath, "you have here all my acts and confessions, for which I must die. It is all falsehood and invention, so help me God. . . . They never cease to torture until one says something. . . . If God sends no means of bringing the truth to light, our whole kindred will be burnt." And indeed he said no more than the truth. As the rage for denunciation spread, whole families were exterminated, whole parishes depopulated. In Trier, in 1585, when the Archbishop had aroused himself, two villages were left with only one female inhabitant apiece. And as the population shrank, so the executioner swelled in prosperity and social status. At Trier he was seen to ride abroad on a fine horse, "like a nobleman of the court, dressed in silver and gold, while his wife vied with noble ladies in dress and luxury." At Schongau in Bavaria he rode about in state with his wife, two servants, and a supply of needles to prick as witches ever more and more victims.

But if, as Spee wrote, it was torture that filled Europe with witches, it would be idle to pretend that all denunciations or confessions came from torture alone. Many witches were undoubtedly impelled by exhibitionism. This was largely true of young girls, some of whom were cured by finding real lovers instead of imaginary incubi. Others genuinely believed their own confessions. After all, they might say, who were they to judge? Old and feeble, undernourished and half-demented, these poor women hated their neighbors with peasant rancor and were hated by them in turn. They lived in a world of malice and delusion, wished to cast spells, dreamed of night-flying and the Devil, and would gladly have served Antichrist, if he existed, to oppose the Christian society which they felt was mobilized against them. When the highest and most learned authorities gravely assured them that all these things were real and could be proved out of books, who were they to dissent? They allowed clergymen and judges to give form and detail to their vague hankerings, their half-felt experiences. And so, even without torture, they confessed. But their confessions rested ultimately on torture all the same. It was because thousands had been tortured into saying they were witches, that the mythology had been built up and now seemed so certain that other thousands, without torture, confessed in tune.

Torture and mythology, the pincers and the book, these were the essential machinery of the European witch craze. Out of hallucination and suggestion they created a terrible empire of darkness which then acquired a life and momentum of its own, independent of outside forces. By the mid-seventeenth century the documentation was so immense, the evidence so complete, the

authorities so confident in their mutual corroboration, the penalties of nonconformity so great, that the return to sanity might well have seemed impossible. A new church had been established, more universal than Catholicism or Protestantism, and all the forces of tradition, custom, discipline, and vested interest joined to sustain it. How could skepticism or sense prevail against so powerful a system? Even a challenge seemed impossible. The thing, it must have seemed, was final. It had come to stay.

So weak men must have argued. So they always do, against any prevalent folly. And yet, as it happened, they were wrong. Even in the hour of triumph the monstrous system began to crumble; now here, now there, the opening cracks appeared. It was in the 1640's that the persecution reached its height in England. Those were the days when Matthew Hopkins, the notorious "witch-finder general," spread terror all through East Anglia, and the greatest holocaust of witches ever known in England—twenty-nine in a batch—took place at the Chelmsford Assizes. And yet within a few

Thunder and lightning, hail and rain are stirred into a wild tempest by a witch riding on a galloping goat.

years the reaction set in. Quite suddenly the tide began to ebb: the few English executions between 1660 and 1685 are trivial last exceptions to a new rule. In France it is the same: witch burning was already in decline when Colbert, in 1673, abolished the charge of *sorcellerie sabbatique*. In Geneva, once so ferocious, the last witch was executed in 1652. The aristocratic cities were emancipated first: popular prejudices were less easy to conquer, especially in rural areas. In the early 1660's there were new outbreaks in backward countries: in Swe-

den, released from royal control; in Scotland and Lorraine, released from English and French occupation. In all three countries the old clergy—Lutheran, Calvinist, and Catholic—had suddenly recovered power. But their victories were short-lived. In general, throughout Europe, the climate of opinion has changed. The old laws may remain on the statute book, the old beliefs linger in school and cloister, but the old power has gone. Even in Germany, where the prince-bishops burned away in corners for another century, the scale of operation is insignificant: the Archbishop of Salzburg's bonfire of ninety-seven witches, in 1679, is the last of the great burnings. The empire of darkness has begun to rot inwardly. The clergy are on the defensive, and there is something hysterical in their last, despairing cries: the cry of the odious Bishop Bossuet in France, protesting that an army of 180,000 witches is threatening all Europe—"I wish they could all be put in one body, all burned at once in one fire"; the protest of the Scottish ministers, in 1736, against that "national sin," the repeal of the witch laws by parliament "contrary to the express laws of God"; the lament, in England, of John Wesley that "the infidels have hooted witchcraft out of the world." Well might they lament. They were defeated. The laity had won. The Enlightenment was at hand.

How did it happen? How does it happen that a closed ideological system, seemingly watertight, self-preserving and self-perpetuating, and fortified with multiple interests, suddenly weakens and crumbles? The question is of obvious general interest. It is of particular interest today, when such systems have been newly built up among us, have become the orthodoxy of the learned, the piety of the devout, and have led, in once civilized countries, to wholesale purges for crimes scarcely less ridiculous than those once analyzed and defined by Rémy and Del Rio, Carpzov and Perkins. In order to answer this question it may be well to consider first the forces that worked against the witch mania, even at its height. For even then there were restraints that prevented it from further expansion. These were of two kinds. First, there was internal discipline, the discipline of the clergy. Secondly, there was external doubt, the doubt of the laity.

The discipline was effective first. At first, indeed, it was the most that could be hoped for. And the only force that could discipline the persecution was the same force that had originally launched it: the Inquisition. It was in Italy and Spain, the centers of the Roman and Spanish Inquisition, that the monstrous doctrines had been formulated; it was there too that they were most firmly controlled. In a memorable chapter of his *History of the Inquisition in Spain,* Lea himself pointed out how that hideous engine of intellectual and racial tyranny yet, by its "wisdom and firmness," held the witch mania down. In this as in other respects it kept Spain in the ignorance and bliss of the tenth century. In Italy the Roman Inquisition was only a little behind. The phenomena were the same as elsewhere, but the attitude of authority was different. Not only was the Inquisition stricter in its definition of witchcraft: sometimes it also tamed the heresy by incorporating it into orthodoxy. The Roman Church has always known how to do this. In the Dark Ages it converted pagan gods into Christian saints; in the Middle Ages it converted its radicals, its Anabaptists, into new orders of monks or friars; and now it did much the same with sorcery. In the Mediterranean lands those who supposed themselves levitated into the air were not burned as witches but canonized as saints. Of course this did not mean that the mythology was discredited; far from it. The Catholic Church clung fast to the belief in witches. But action at least was regulated. Perhaps it is no accident that the period of English history when the persecution, though not intellectually undermined, was most firmly controlled, was the period of Arminian government under Charles I and Archbishop Laud—the nearest Protestant England ever came to an Inquisition.

Thus something was owed to clerical discipline. The Inquisition burnt scholars, saints, and Jews, but it was scrupulous about old women. And yet in the long run this leads us nowhere. At best, clerical discipline could only have limited the persecution to "true witches." The intellectual foundations of the persecution remained intact. To end it, it must be proved that there were no true witches, and this meant an intellectual revolution. It did not, of course, mean a Protestant revolution: for the Prot-

estant clergy, as we have seen, were just as bad as the Catholic, the Calvinist ministers as the Dominican friars. What was needed was an anticlerical revolution, a revolt of lay reason against the new cosmology of the Church. But such a revolution was in fact easier in Protestant than in Catholic countries, because in Protestant countries the clergy, in general, had less power. The Reformation had owed its original success to lay support; and where it had prevailed, and where there was an educated middle class to consolidate its victory, the laity saw to it that the new clergy never obtained quite the power of the old. Moreover, in Protestant countries there were no religious orders—those formidable religious armies which, while they evangelized among the masses, could also mobilize the prejudices of the masses against the occasional liberalism even of popes and bishops. Thus the educated laity, if they existed, were far stronger, far freer in Protestant than in Catholic countries. Being free, they could accept intellectual revolutions which their own clergy resisted. They could accept the revolution against Aristotle, the revolution of Copernicus and Galileo. They could also accept the revolution against witches, the revolution of the Sadducees. The revolu-

Unsuspecting victims are first put to sleep with devilish potions and later poisoned by well-dressed witches.

tionaries themselves might be Catholics, as Copernicus and Galileo were, but that made no difference. The base even of their revolution had to be found in Protestant, unclerical lands. So the work of Galileo, condemned in Rome, was published in Protestant Strasbourg. Thus it was in Protestant Holland, the first country to abandon witch trials and witch burnings, that the under-

lying theory itself, long secretly doubted, was first publicly overthrown. It was overthrown by Balthasar Bekker who, in 1691, "struck at the roots of the terror by doubting the Devil himself."

So in the days of its expansion the witch craze ran up against a double movement of restraint. In the south, clerical discipline pressed on its surface; in the north, lay reason undermined its heart. The importance of these restraints is clear if we look, for a moment, at areas where neither was effective: where the clergy had power but not discipline and where the laity lacked education and social strength. Such conditions can be found in both Catholic and Protestant lands: in Catholic lands without centralized church law, in Protestant lands without a strong, educated middle class.

In Catholic lands the obvious instance is the region north of the Alps. There customary law gave all power to local rulers and those rulers were Catholics without restraint. So Lorraine and Burgundy, Bavaria and the Rhineland, the prince-bishoprics of Germany and the Catholic cantons of Switzerland were the classic lands of witchcraft. There the greatest persecutions took place, there the great encyclopedias were published, thence the successive waves of hatred and fear rolled out over Europe. On this geographical fact all were agreed, believers and unbelievers alike. It is notorious, wrote Spee, that witches abound in Germany above all other countries. In Burgundy, protested the magistrates of a clerical enclave, "the evil grows daily and this wretched breed multiplies everywhere." It was in Germany, said Bossuet, that the whole population was kept busy burning witches, in Switzerland that villages were entirely depopulated by executions, in Lorraine that the traveler could see "thousands and thousands of stakes," the only means of keeping down this pest "that multiplies on the earth like caterpillars in our gardens." Clerical power, lack of legal centralization, absence of an educated middle class, and torture—all the conditions were fulfilled to make these old "prince-bishoprics" the last stronghold of the European witch mania.

In Protestant lands the classic examples come from the Calvinist theocracies in those two underdeveloped countries, Stuart Scotland and colonial New England. The

Scottish clergy enjoyed their last great witch hunt in the 1660's; their New England brethren a whole generation later, in 1692. But the basic elements are the same. New England society was a society without, as yet, a strong educated laity; its clergy, the Calvinist oligarchy, was sufficiently powerful to dictate orthodoxy and fan hatred, but it lacked the centralized machinery of law to control the passions aroused; and if there was no legal torture, at least there were equivalent inducements: "hardships and torments" for those who would not confess, life and liberty for those who would. So, when the witch craze broke out at Salem, there was much to extend it, little to stop it. The clerical leaders, delighted by the evidence produced by a few hysterical girls for their own theories, first beat the drum ecclesiastic and then failed to control their followers. "I have set myself," wrote the Reverend Cotton Mather complacently, "to countermine the whole plot of the Devil against New England, in every branch of it." No doubt, he admitted, evil spirits would be exasperated by his words, just as the Jewish Sadducees had been by those of Christ; but he would not stop his crusade for that. Nor did he. In the end, when two hundred people had been accused, one hundred and fifty imprisoned, and twenty-nine executed on the "spectral evidence" of their demented neighbors who claimed to have seen them at the Sabbath, even he took alarm. But still he reserved his real hatred not for the executions but for a "vile volume" produced by "a very wicked sort of Sadducee": a volume which his father, the respected president of Harvard College, caused to be burned in the college yard. This vile volume was the protest of a layman, the merchant Robert Calef, who, with his fellow-merchant, Thomas Brattle, deserves to be remembered as the herald of lay reason in America; and it had been published safely outside clerical control, in London.

Thus, after two centuries, the lay spirit triumphed again, and belief in witchcraft, intellectually discredited, deprived of its organization and sanctions, no longer sure of the assent of rulers and judges, sank back again into its original, its permanent character: it remained, and remains, what it had been in antiquity and the Dark Ages, a congeries of peasant superstitions. By the

eighteenth century the clergy, Catholic and Protestant alike (all but their lunatic fringe), quietly forgot the doctrines they still did not dare to disown. For the clergy too, by the eighteenth century, had become laicized. Their extremists—the Dominicans, the Calvinists—had fought hard. Where they had held power, where the laity had been weak or uneducated, and the traditional rulers—princes, bishops, or town governors—had been dependent on them, there they had prevailed. But where they had been weak or divided, as in Protestant Holland and England, and even in Catholic France (which was also, to its intellectual salvation, Jansenist France), there lay reason had found a base, the Sadducees had

Compendium Maleficarum, GUAZZO, LONDON 1929

The burned remains of hanged disinterred corpses provide the powerful fuel to propel a witch's flying stick.

published their books, and the forces of orthodoxy had been gradually divided. Even within the clerical body there had appeared "liberal" clergy, allies of the laity and strong by that alliance, the heirs of the old humanist, Erasmian clergy who, in the sixteenth century, had been so remorselessly snuffed out. Once that division had happened, what a prospect opened! Having found a base, the rot spread. Iron curtains could not keep it back; for it is impossible, in a prosperous, competitive, literate world, to keep even a clergy, even a bureaucracy, even a praetorian guard permanently divorced from the laity—provided the laity have equal opportunities of self-support and independent education.

And this, it seems to me, is the ultimate comfort in this squalid story of collective, organized lunacy and cruelty. The theorists of power maintain that by creating a separate caste in society—a Party, or the Elect

—and arming it with a doctrine, an ideology, they can make both slavery and nonsense permanent. "I am persuaded," Bertrand Russell, our greatest rationalist once sadly confessed, "that there is absolutely no limit to the absurdities that can, by government action, come to be generally believed. Give me an adequate army, with power to provide it with more pay and better food than falls to the lot of the average man, and I will undertake, within thirty years, to make the majority of the population believe that two and two are three, that water freezes when it gets hot and boils when it gets cold, or any other nonsense that might seem to serve the interest of the State." The history of the European witch craze shows that this can indeed be done—for a time. When we read of men like Bodin and Rémy—by all accounts liberal, humane, learned men—hanging and burning old women with the conscientious zeal of saviors of society, we realize how completely an artificial system of nonsense, once established, can take possession even of thinking, rational men; and we are tempted to wonder whether perhaps today our minds may not be equally imprisoned, though in other prisons, from which only the cranks whom we persecute will ultimately save us. For it is not only churches that manufacture myths and win assent to them: bureaucracies, political parties, general staffs can do the same. On the other hand, the history of the witch craze also shows the limitations of delusion. Perhaps in an economically undeveloped country isolated from the outer world and absolutely controlled by the priests of the myth, it may be possible to fool all the people all the time. But if political power requires economic development and economic development requires an educated laity, able to listen to ideas from outside, and if there is an outside world where different ideas can find a base, then ultimately the solidarity even of such a party can be rotted; lay reason will infiltrate even into the clergy; sense will prevail.

H. R. Trevor-Roper, Regius Professor of Modern History at Christ Church, Oxford, writes frequently for HORIZON. *His most recent subject was "The Sudden End of the Renaissance" (September, 1959).*

A MEMORANDUM

From: Jonathan Swift

To: Cliff Robinson, President of
the National Association of
Secondary-School Principals

Subject: A Modest Proposal for Pre-
venting the Children of
America from Being a Burden
to their Parents or Country

By WILLIAM HARLAN HALE

Sir: It hath been discovered to me in this Place, from which I continue to observe the Fortunes of Men, although happily removed from them, that the People of America are pursuing novel Methods in teaching their Young, and that the School-men whom you have the Honour of leading play a large part in this ingenious Effort. You have long abandoned Flogging, preferring to encourage the Root of Nature rather than apply the Branch that was so long England's chief instrument of inculcating Learning. You have since generally abandoned much unprofitable Learning as well: first Greek, then Latin, and then—if I read the publick Prints aright—often the study of *English* also. I am sensible that this may be the final consequence of the American Revolution. It arouses no ill temper in me; on the contrary, Sir, I applaud your Consistency in casting off the Past.

But have you cast off enough of it? I cannot but observe a certain Disagreement among yourselves in America as to your Schools, your Teachers, and your Young, and this I can ascribe only to Hesitation. Why should this be? Have you not performed an immense advance over the accumulated Dross, Obscuration, and rigid *postulata* of other Ages? You have long cast out Rhetoric, Moral Philosophy, and even those twin tyrants, History and Geography, replacing them by what your Guardians of the schools call "Social Studies" (though I vow I myself often thought of History as less than social, and of the Earth's compass as embracing more than Man).

And you have gone further. You may not teach Roman History; but you have endow'd your teaching Institutions with the greatest Gymnasia and Stadia seen since Roman times. Rome gave its young commoners Sports and Circuses, and sought not to educate any but the sons of good Family; in America, you once set out to educate all, but today I am inform'd that you instruct the high and the lowly alike more in Play than Learning. You have constructed a Philosophy which holds that Education is but Adjustment to Life, and that the Young learn best by doing, which I take to mean exercising the Limbs and Spirit far from the mouldy dust of Libraries. And the Press hath it that you now instruct your

DRAWING BY MILTON GLASER

Charges in the lively arts of Homemaking, Cosmetics, and the Technic of Camping, Cookery, and something whose meaning escapeth me, "Dating." Your own Schoolmen's Association in particular, when these Innovations were traduced by scurrilous Weeklies and crabbed Antiquarians unable to appreciate the full Promise of Liberty, has struck back boldly at the Critics. Yet, with all this Spirit of Freedom about, you in America still labour under a crushing Burden of Schoolhouses, although they are of less and less Utility, and you complain that their Costs grow yearly. What a paradoxical condition of Man, to remain enslaved to the Past when in near sight of his Millennium!

Though I have long passed into that Place where—as I wrote in my epitaph—my indignation can no longer lacerate my heart, I remain the Enemy of all Oppression, Pretense, and human Vanity. Having turned my Thoughts, for many Years, to the Follies of the Learned, I now offer for your consideration a Proposal that may resolve your Difficulties, silence your Opponents, and lead to a unique Fulfillment. It is more modest than the Proposal I once offered for the Disposition of the Children of Ireland, the times then being of far greater Disorder and Distress. My present thought is simply that publick Educators in America, having so widely abandoned Education in all but Name, now draw the logical Conclusion and discontinue it altogether, closing the Schools as Relicts of the Past and transferring their remaining Exercises to Playgrounds and Playhouses.

The Advantages of this Proposal are obvious and many. It would lift a crushing Burden of Taxation. It would relieve Parents who are now filled with Melancholy at the Failure of their Children to do better in their Studies, or even to learn to *read*, from further Anxiety on this account. It would release many Teachers, now bound to lives of Penury, to more promising Employment. It would, by removing the Temptations of Literacy, eliminate the Incursions of foreign Propaganda against which your Statesmen have inveigh'd—and it would turn out the Scribblers of your popular sheets upon other pastures, too, thereby augmenting the world's useful Labour Force. Above all, it would surely serve to usher in that entire Equality which has ever been the ideal of your Nation's

greatest Philosophers, yet for the full Realization of which the Means have until now remained wanting.

'Twill be objected that this Proposal would arrest the advancement of higher American Talent, and, second, that an American Elite of Brains is now particularly needed to equal that of *Russia's*. Both arguments I find so sophistical as to be unworthy of a great Democracy at its Prime. For what higher Democratic talent is there than to Identify, as your Schoolmen say, with the "Group," which I take to mean the Commonalty. In my Years I wrote of the Apostles of pretentious Learning as haughty, useless Fellows engaged upon such Ventures as trying to extract sunbeams from cucumbers and constructing machines for the capture of Owls. You have broken the Tyranny of the overeducated. Was ever a Thought so craven express'd as that a great People, so near total Freedom from old Frippery and Encrustation, should now follow like a Cockle-boat in the wake of academical Muscovy?

What immense Possibilities would arise, if my Proposal were acted upon! The Pursuit of Happiness, long profess'd as an American goal, would now be made complete, particularly for the tender Young on the Threshold of Life. Schools would be left as mere *Museums*, giving mute testimony, as Monuments, Tombs, and Catacombs now do, to Man's Struggles and Burdens in the Past. That Past, whose example teacheth little but the prevalence of Evil, would be dismiss'd from further Consideration, and a fresh and innocent Beginning made. The ponderous study of the Fate of Man—a fate admitted to be unknowable even by the foremost Authorities—would no longer detain us from more useful and pleasant Occupations. I have long held that Wisdom, unless you bite carefully, is but a Nut which may cost you a Tooth, and repay you with nothing but a Worm. We could now return, Sir, to a State of Nature. And what Pedants of Moscow could long survive in any Contest with a new, happy Breed of American noble Savages, so unlike the Yahoos of my *Gulliver?*

I profess I myself have not the least Personal Interest one way or the other in promoting this Cause, having written my best-known Work for the Discernment of Elders, only to find it long since reduced to a Plaything about Pygmies and Giants for the Diversion of Children.

On February 12, 1934, a day of extreme political tension in France, with a general strike under way and tempers rising, a Socialist official engaged a Paris construction worker in casual conversation. What the country needed in such times, said the worker, was a *real* leader —"a fellow like Gide." The incident was reported in the *Nouvelle Revue Française,* and it illustrates as nothing else could the exceptional position the French writer occupies in the minds of his countrymen. That André Gide, of all literary men perhaps the least suited to the barricades, should have been honored in this way simply adds an ironic note to an otherwise earnest situation. To appreciate how very different we are from the French in this respect, we have only to imagine a New York street repairman suggesting William Faulkner for the White House.

It would seem that Shelley's remark about poets being the unacknowledged legislators of mankind does not apply to the French. Among them the poet, as well as the novelist, the

The Writer as the Conscience of France

Voltaire's and Victor Hugo's tradition continues in the work of Albert Camus

playwright, the critic, and—most French of occupations— the man of letters, is not only acknowledged as a lawgiver but esteemed to a degree that professional politicians have always envied. One result of the high value set on writing in France is that it is difficult to find a French political leader since the Revolution without at least one book to his credit, if only his memoirs, or any who would not prefer, at least secretly, to be known to history for his style rather than for his boulevards, penal code, or tax reforms. Certainly Charles de Gaulle, whatever his other achievements, will be remembered for his exemplary prose.

In no other country has the great writer received such adulation or the lesser one such respect. To write in France is to make a stake for glory, and *la gloire* can be heady indeed. Here is Maurice Barrès describing the funeral of Victor Hugo on May 31, 1885: "The scene had to be seen to be believed. The coffin lifted in the black darkness, and the greenish glare of the street lamps showing livid on the Imperial gateway,

By RICHARD GILMAN

and reflected in the breastplates of the cavalrymen who, torch in hand, were keeping back the crowd. A mass of people eddied and flowed from as far away as the Place de la Concorde [the ceremonies were taking place at the Arc de Triomphe], pressing forward against the barrier of terrified horses to within two hundred yards of the catafalque. There was, in them, a wild wonder at the knowledge that they had made a god. . . ."

Next day two million persons are said to have followed the hearse to the Panthéon, where the poet's remains were interred among generals, statesmen, and a good many of his fellow writers. Four years earlier Hugo had been granted a foretaste of this posthumous transfiguration. As he entered his eightieth year a national holiday had been proclaimed and six hundred thousand of his fellow citizens had passed in an interminable parade beneath his window, shouting their homage as he smiled down on them from his balcony, and carrying placards that defined the exact position he held among them: master, leader, and demigod.

It is true that France has not since witnessed a spectacle quite like these two. Hugo, partly because France had not yet had a Shakespeare and partly because of the special political circumstances of his era, carried a greater symbolic weight than has any French writer since his death. But the apotheosis he received has its minor counterparts in all periods of French history. At a performance of his play *Irène*, the 84-year-old Voltaire watched from a box while his bust was solemnly crowned with laurel on the stage. When Paul Valéry, a notably aloof and austere poet, died in 1945, he was given a state funeral and was mourned by immense crowds very few of whose members had ever read a line he wrote. Ten years later the death of Paul Claudel, another poet who had placed his hopes of reward somewhat further along in eternity, was the occasion for impressive services at Notre Dame and a nation's grieving for its great dead son.

This exalted position of the writer in France has sometimes led to a temptation on his part to grasp power at its material

All Paris stands silent as Victor Hugo's funeral cortege turns into the Place de la Concorde

root. Poets and novelists, along with historians, philosophers, naturalists, and authors of treatises on cooking and millinery, have continually tried their hand at politics. Not many have been elected, and few of these have distinguished themselves in office. They have tended to ignore the realities of public business in favor of exercises in grandiloquence (Henry James tells of reading Hugo's "windy sublimities" in the evening paper) or visionary schemes for national regeneration. Still, the point is that no one in France finds it disconcerting for a writer to stand for deputy or senator or to accept appointive office. In our own time two premiers, Léon Blum and Edouard Herriot, had achieved literary fame before entering politics; Claudel, St.-John Perse, Jean Giraudoux, and Jacques Maritain all served as diplomats; Romain Gary is at present the French consul-general in Los Angeles; and Malraux is a member of De Gaulle's cabinet.

In reality the relationship between literature and politics in France is a more subtle one. The French do not demand from their writers achievements on the level of practical politics, although they are always ready to welcome these. What they ask of literature is that it serve as both judge and creator of values, political and otherwise, and that the writer be prepared to function as seer and arbiter, expert in the higher sense and trustee of the national conscience. Literature, Hugo wrote, is "civilization itself," and nowhere is this dictum believed more fervently than in France, a nation which has been known to claim for its own civilization exclusive right to the word. For us the novel, the drama, poetry, or criticism may be many things, from delight to instruction, but we do not usually ask them to bear such a weight of significance as do the French. Especially, we are not accustomed to finding in literature our most profound, and even exclusive, guide to life.

The French look to their writers as other peoples look to their preachers, statesmen, or, in some contemporary cases, men of business. The word that best defines the French writer's role is *moralist*, by which is meant something much deeper than the qualities we ordinarily attach to it. It has little to do with the delivery of sermons or indeed with anything directly ethical. By moralist the French mean the man who has a moral vision, who sees into the nature of existence, defines the human situation, gives form to it, and offers, at the great crises of the spirit, alternatives, bridges, transcendencies. In one way or another, however explicitly they may reject such a role, however self-contained is their commitment or purely aesthetic their engagement, all important French writers—at least since Montaigne—have been moralists of this kind. There is a direct line of unmistakable ones, running from Pascal down to Malraux and Saint-Exupéry, but Balzac, Baudelaire, Proust, Gide, and René Char will be found to qualify as well.

Although, in France, simply to write with any degree of seriousness is to participate in the ambience of authority established by the tradition of letters—so that far more atten-

tion is paid there to newspaper columnists, critics, and the obiter dicta of professors than is the case here—the most meaningful influence upon day-to-day political and social life is exercised by those whose reputations stem from more purely creative sources. It is the degree to which a writer has been able to transcend his times that his judgments on them are respected: a paradox that reveals how thoroughly the French dispense with our distinction between the practical and the visionary. It is not too much to say that in the long run France receives even her most utilitarian lessons from her classic novels, plays, and poems.

Voltaire in the Calas case or Zola in the Dreyfus affair would scarcely have accomplished much had not their indignation and demand for justice been given resonance and majesty by their immense prestige as creators. In this sense, the direct effect that great writers have upon French issues is like an overflow from their nontopical work; when they speak out, it is with a voice strengthened by a proprietary concern with permanent values and echoing like the conscience of the people themselves.

Hugo was certainly indulging his taste for egoistic bombast when, from his refuge in Brussels, he told a correspondent, "It is not I, sir, who have been outlawed, but liberty; it is not I who have been exiled, but France." But at the same time he was telling the French people what most of them wished to have said about their situation under Louis Napoleon and what they were more than willing to accord Hugo the right to say.

In the same way, when Gide published the journals of his travels in the Congo in the late twenties, he acted as the conscience of France. It was his stature as an artist that made it impossible for the government to ignore the charges he brought against the colonial administration, or, more accurately, against the great concessionary companies which Gide found exploiting and abusing the natives they employed and which the administration was unable or unwilling to control. The reforms set in motion, at least in part by Gide's accusations, provide a not untypical illustration of the power of literature in France to pierce the hide of officialdom and bring about changes in the structure and exercise of authority.

François Mauriac is another man whose eminence as a writer gives edge and forcefulness to his critiques of national policy as they impinge upon moral issues. Within the last few years Mauriac has been involved, through his weekly newspaper column, with such *causes célèbres* as the question of brutality on the part of the French army in Algeria and the earlier affair of a soldier sentenced to five years in solitary confinement for distributing leaflets protesting the war in Indochina. In the latter instance, Mauriac played a leading role in forcing a review and subsequent mitigation of the sentence, while in the former he continues at the center of an increasingly agonized national examination of conscience.

What of the writer who does not declare himself on specific questions, who works in isolation at his craft (as far as that is possible in France), secreting a vision divorced from immediacies? His creation will then enter silently into the stream of national consciousness; it will have a subterranean effect, and even for those who never come directly upon it, it will serve, along with the name of its creator, as an emblem of man's will toward clarity, inner triumph, and the shaping of destiny through mind and imagination. The French, as we know, do not have to read their poets in order to adore them.

But more frequently, and increasingly since the Romantics, the writer in France has presented that double image of timeless originator and commentator on the actual (even surrealism was in one sense a "comment") that Frenchmen regard as the completeness of literary existence. If today there is no French author whose reflection from either glass fixes the gaze of his contemporaries the way Chateaubriand's did during the First Empire or Hugo's during the Third Republic, or even Gide's quite recently, there is little question that the man who comes closest to doing it is the astonishingly fecund Algerian-born novelist, playwright, and essayist, Albert Camus.

In Camus many Frenchmen see converging all the chief strands of their current moral, intellectual, and aesthetic concerns; his work is coming to embody for them the main elements of the spiritual crisis through which France has been passing. That the rest of the world should so largely share his

countrymen's esteem for Camus is, of course, a testimony to the more than local validity of art, but also to France's continuing pre-eminence in the dominion of the mind: she is still the nation from which we expect portents, revelations, and prescriptions for renascence.

No one has written a more eloquent tribute to Camus' hold on the imagination of France than Jean-Paul Sartre: ". . . you bore within yourself all the conflicts of our time and went beyond them because of the ardor with which you lived them. You were a real *person*, the most complex and the richest, the last and most gifted of the heirs of Chateaubriand. . . . You had all the luck and all the merits, bringing to a sense of greatness a passionate sense of beauty, to the joy of living the sense of death. How we loved you then."

If Sartre employs the past tense in speaking of Camus, it is because by the time this encomium appeared—in the August, 1952, number of Sartre's *Les Temps Modernes*—the two men had quarreled bitterly. Yet to any Frenchman who is not blinded by either political or literary prejudice the praise retains its accuracy. Historically, it renders exactly the quality of the enthusiasm so many men had for Camus during the last years of the war and the immediate postwar period. From the moment he made his entrance, both triumphant and shy, upon the literary scene he seemed to them the incarna-

Voltaire's bust is crowned with laurel at the Théâtre Français, 1778

DRAWINGS BY ARNO STERNGLASS

tion of everything they had been waiting for: he was a writer who combined the memory of suffering with an articulation of hope, confident thought with a recognition of chaos, a love of beauty with an unflinching awareness of tragedy.

That Camus, or any writer, should have been awaited with such fervor is a measure both of the degree to which literature perennially matters to the French and of the extraordinary circumstances of the epoch in which he came to their attention. Camus' first book, *The Stranger*, was published in 1942, at perhaps the lowest point of French morale under the German occupation. The novel was in no way a political testament; there was nothing in it of the rallying cry, nor was it a parable aimed at the conqueror in the manner of certain other literary productions that had managed to circulate under the noses of the not-too-perceptive Nazis.

Yet this short novel—clinical, pure, with an almost unbearable honesty—struck a chord in readers starved for authentic words and for hope no matter how austere. The "Stranger" of its title is a young office worker who heedlessly shoots an Arab on a bright Algerian beach. It is a nonpolitical, not even passionate crime—a meaningless act of violence induced by "the sun." But while he is in prison, awaiting execution, Camus' Stranger discovers the minimum ground of existence: that all men alike are condemned to die. To face this certain fact is the beginning of mastery over life's terrors and unreason: "That, no doubt, was all I had; but at least that certainty was something I could get my teeth into—just as it had got its teeth into me. . . . I'd passed my life in a certain way, and I might have passed it in a different way if I'd felt like it. I'd acted thus, and I hadn't acted otherwise; I hadn't done *x*, whereas I had done *y* or *z*. And what did that mean? That, all the time, I'd been waiting for this present moment, for that dawn, tomorrow's or another day's, which was to justify me." In all this, Frenchmen found a text for the times.

When the same year Camus' *The Myth of Sisyphus* appeared, his reputation grew. It was a set of essays that reinterpreted in a startling way the Greek myth of the man condemned eternally to roll a rock uphill. Nothing could be more hopeless and bereft of meaning on the face of it, yet Camus declared that it was precisely in the acceptance of his task that Sisyphus could find justification and even happiness. "I leave Sisyphus at the foot of the mountain! One always finds one's burden again. But Sisyphus teaches the higher fidelity that negates the gods and raises rocks. . . . The struggle itself toward the

Albert Camus

heights is enough to fill a man's heart. One must imagine Sisyphus happy."

Camus' philosophy, as he expressed it in *The Stranger* and *The Myth of Sisyphus*, rested on the recognition that the human condition is intolerable because it eludes our reasoning. The world is not absurd—this is what separates Camus from the existentialists—but we *feel* it to be. The certainty of death undermines all our hopes and privileges. Our nostalgia for meaning confronts an irrational, silent universe—so that we are led to conclude that life is meaningless and therefore without value. In these early works Camus saw a possible victory in the mere acknowledgment of this truth—in admitting the absurdity of life but in persevering, like Sisyphus, in the face of what seems unacceptable. Life may be unreasonable, but he persuades us that it is infinitely valuable, and that any attempt to evade it is a defeat.

Interest in Camus was strengthened by the subsequent wartime publication of two plays, *Caligula* and *The Misunderstanding*, which exemplified new aspects of his search for meaning within the dilemmas of existence. Before that he had been known to a small group within the Resistance and admired by a much larger audience for his unsigned editorials in the clandestine newspaper *Combat*. Such underground journals as *Combat* played a significant role in the French struggle against the Germans. In fact, the literary aspect of the Resistance took precedence in many minds over the political one; for a writer to use his talents for Vichy or the Germans was considered, for example, almost a greater act of treason than any similar action on the part of a politician.

With the liberation of Paris, Camus' name appeared on *Combat*'s masthead as its editorial director. In those surging days, when a rebirth seemed to be awaiting France, his voice came to rival Sartre's as an enunciator of French expectations and possibilities, but it was even more persuasive as an awakener of consciences and interpreter of the anguish the nation had collectively experienced. In France someone is forever having to sum up the past so that the future may be made viable for the rest.

It was this sort of recapitulation that Camus undertook in some of the impassioned editorials he wrote during the postwar period. In one of them he touched on the deepest moral and psychic wound that France, together with the rest of Europe, had suffered—one that only a new and stringent kind of honesty such as he was beginning to provide could heal. "Something in us," he wrote, "was destroyed by the spectacle of the years through which we have just lived. And that something is the eternal confidence of man which always led him to believe that one could elicit human reactions from another man by speaking the language of humanity."

This "language of humanity" received a partial reconstruction in Camus' journalistic writings, but it was necessarily tentative and skeletal there. It was in the novels, plays, and essays which Camus began to produce in a steady rhythm—*The Plague* (1947), *State of Siege* (1948), *The Just Assassins*

(1950), *The Rebel* (1951)—that his public came to discover the more complex, permanent, and unfettered qualities of his thought and sensibility: his vigor and joyousness, irony and bitter humor, his preoccupation with the problem of freedom, of the relations between means and ends, and of man as the creator of his own values. As each new work appeared, an event in a nation accustomed to such events, the conviction grew among sensitive Frenchmen that they possessed a true inheritor of their accumulated literary resources, revivified by a greatly original mind.

The Plague has been called by one of Camus' most perceptive critics, Germaine Brée, "a great novel, the most disturbing, most moving novel yet to have come out of the chaos of mid-century." It is the story of a pestilence that comes to afflict the city of Oran, cutting it off from the outside world and converting it into a stage upon which a metaphysical drama is enacted. From the first appearance of dying rats in the streets, the inhabitants react with varying degrees of apathy, disbelief, horror, and—as the plague spreads—despair. But ultimately their hold on life is restored. What has saved them is the determination of a small group of men to combat the plague with every human resource, since they are aware of its double character as physical evil and symbol of a deeper malaise. Their opposition to it is located within a primal will to live and to assert the dignity of living.

What might have been simply an allegory in which life triumphs over death, or good over evil, becomes, through its wealth of realized incident and characterization, a major, complex image of man's condition and possibilities. Philosophically, too, the novel marks an advance over *The Stranger*. There man's fate was seen as unfolding against an unfathomable universe, in terrible clarity but in isolation and submissiveness. *The Plague* re-enters the world of men in their need for one another, as they forge and explore a solidarity in the face of evil. Love of life rises up in its pages, together with unwavering faith in man's capacity to establish values within his own condition.

In *The Rebel*, his longest philosophical work, Camus' theme of the apparent absurdity of life and man's search for meaning in the face of it attains a new dimension. Here he examines the implications of revolt. When a slave revolts against his master, it is to obtain a measure of freedom or a measure of justice for himself. But political revolutions, with their tendency toward excess, go further; it is their demand for "absolute freedom" and "absolute justice" that has culminated so terribly in the totalitarianisms of our day. Our hope, Camus says, lies in the notion of *limits*. Applied to his ideas on revolution, it means resistance to the temptation of the absolute. In the midst of the necessary struggle for justice, respect for freedom—the freedom of others—should set a boundary beyond which we refuse to go; at the same time, we must hold to the idea of justice whenever we are tempted to pursue freedom too far.

Camus published no major work from 1951 until 1956,

when *The Fall* appeared. This novel, or *recit*, caused tremendous interest, disappointing some readers because of its apparent withdrawal into cynicism and moral solitude, but appearing to others as a deepening of Camus' journey into the nature of guilt and innocence, conscience and responsibility. It is the most directly religious of Camus' books, not in its avowals or affirmations—Camus remains a steadfast atheist—but in the fact that it takes up with utmost rigor those fundamental questions to which religion traditionally addresses itself.

The next year Camus published *Exile and the Kingdom*, a volume of short stories built mostly around moments of experience in which the need and difficulty of commitment to life is brought home. The same year, 1957, saw the awarding of the Nobel Prize to Camus for his "important literary work which illuminates, with penetrating purposiveness, the problems of the human conscience in the contemporary world." He was France's ninth Nobel literary winner, and at forty-three the second youngest man to have received the honor.

Obeying the rhythm which runs throughout French literature, and which is particularly pronounced in his case, Camus has in recent years supplemented his novels and plays by an occasional return to journalism and the topical essay. One matter that closely concerns him is the Algerian question, upon which he has written extensively, pleading for understanding, principle, and patience. Born in a small Algerian town, Camus spent his youth and wrote his first books in Algiers, coming to France only with the advent of the war. All his works bear the marks of his North African origins, though this is especially true of his earlier writings, suffused as they are with an almost pagan love of the sun as well as with a counterbalancing passion for the desert's nude ascetic qualities, the way it reminds man of his spiritual loneliness.

Besides Algeria, he has written on other aspects of French policy, and world developments as they evoke his sympathy, anger, or concern. At present, the wheel having turned round again, he is at work upon a new novel, which many expect to carry him very much further than he has gone.

Although Camus' position in the forefront of French writing seems secure, it is by no means unchallenged. French literary history has a long record of fratricide. From a political or ideological bias, a difference in taste or aesthetic theory, or sometimes from undisguised envy, French writers have flung at each other anathemas that make the literary feuds of other cultures seem genteel and that, incidentally, constitute an important body of writing in themselves. This internecine warfare is not surprising in a country where the word is so highly valued.

The most violent attacks upon Camus have come from Communist or Communist-minded intellectuals. Ideologies have played an increasingly central part in the perennial French debate over the uses of literature, to the point that they have begun to crowd out aesthetic considerations. So committed are almost all French writers to some form of leftist belief that they have been compelled to undergo crucial self-examinations, and harsh public criticism, in relation to their attitude towards Russia, Marxism, and the French Communist Party.

In Camus' case, his guilt in Communist eyes is clear. He has built much of his intellectual program around a condemnation of Marxist thought and Soviet practice, an indictment he began composing after he had abandoned his early hopes for a common cause between the Communists and other left-wing parties in the postwar reshaping of France. But Camus is also a menace in the eyes of the extreme Right, which abhors his insistence upon the end of privilege and the transformation of the moral climate of capitalism.

The longest section of *The Rebel* is a sustained, merciless critique of both the aberrations of Marxist philosophy and the inhuman nature of Soviet power. The book was savagely denounced in the Communist press and in those journals, such as Sartre's *Les Temps Modernes,* whose agonizing tightrope act over the Marxist abyss is one of the wonders of contemporary France. But even before that, Sartre, calling Camus a "lap dog of reaction," had broken with him over the issue of support for the French Communist Party—which Sartre insisted, and until recently contrived to believe, was the workers' best hope, but which Camus saw with growing clarity as their chief betrayer.

That Sartre should have launched as heavy an attack as he did indicates his recognition of the extent to which Camus was displacing him from his position of authority on politico-intellectual matters. At one point they were almost as familiar a coupling as Keats and Shelley or Plato and Aristotle, although the two shared little besides an interest in common problems, and leadership among French intellectuals. The vendetta, a lop-sided affair since Camus seldom replies to Sartre, continues to hold the attention of a great many Frenchmen, who see in it a microcosm of their severest crisis of thought.

In addition to political and ideological detractors, Camus has literary and philosophic ones. There are critics who maintain that his creative work suffers from the suppression of his natural lyricism in favor of the propagation of explicit values. On the other hand, some philosophers have attacked his theoretical writings for their lack of system, their artist's approach to matters of speculative thought. To the latter Camus has replied that he is indeed not a philosopher, but precisely a man who wishes to oppose the abstractions of philosophy and to give thought a basis in experience. The literary objectors he has not answered at all.

Camus is not excessively bothered by the disputes that rage around his head and in his name. What does trouble him is his exposure to one of the more unfortunate aspects of the cult of letters in France. The novelist Julien Gracq has sardonically described the effect *la gloire* can have on the nerves and self-discipline of the literary hero: "For the writers of other countries 'the public' means the glow of little lamps peacefully lit after dinner in anonymous rooms . . . it calls up the bucolic image of a kind of animal spread out over a meadow, peacefully grazing. . . . For the French writer, it is a drug that is always at hand . . . the murmur of an over-stimulated and unstable crowd, the feverish clamor of an eternal stock exchange."

To protect himself from the drug and the clamor, Camus has adopted a brusque and even glacial manner to those whom he suspects of not having a serious purpose in approaching him. Yet he can engage in humor at his own expense, mocking the fashionableness of certain key words in his vocabulary. "I no longer say, even in a casual way, 'how absurd,' " he recently told an interviewer. "There are other terms, too, that always turn up in reference to me: limit, measure. I'll have to renew my adjectives. A tiring job." He also manages to turn aside lightly the persistent claim, or accusation, that he is an existentialist. "Perhaps I'll really have to make up my mind to study existentialism," he once remarked.

The truth is that no schools confine Camus, nor does any analysis exhaust his meanings or possibilities. Perhaps, like Malraux before him, he will turn one day to a totally unexpected form of literature. In France it is even possible to remain a writer without writing, as Rimbaud did, living in the consciousness of his contemporaries after his premature creative death, or Valéry during his seventeen-year silence. So passionately does France hold literature to be man's highest achievement and justification that she can interpret its abandonment by a great practitioner as a sacrificial act which enhances it all the more.

But there is no reason to suppose that Camus will offer this sort of testimony.

What we may expect of him is that, between the demands of the moment and the claims of art, between the hunger for beauty and the limiting sword of ethics, he will continue to find a narrow but saving passage. That is what all great French writers have striven for. No one has more movingly expressed what that endeavor entails than Camus. In his Nobel Prize acceptance speech he spoke of the writer in terms that capture the central qualities of candor, committedness, and ache for immortality that have always distinguished the literature of France. He is, he said, a man "vulnerable and stubborn, unjust and eager for justice, constructing his work without shame or pride within sight of all, constantly torn between pain and beauty, and devoted to extracting from his dual nature the creations he obstinately strives to elevate in the destructive fluctuations of history."

His words constitute a manifesto for himself, for the genius of France, and for the enduring life of art.

Richard Gilman is currently at work on a study of postwar French literature. He has contributed poetry and critical articles to Chicago Review, Pax, *and* Commonweal.

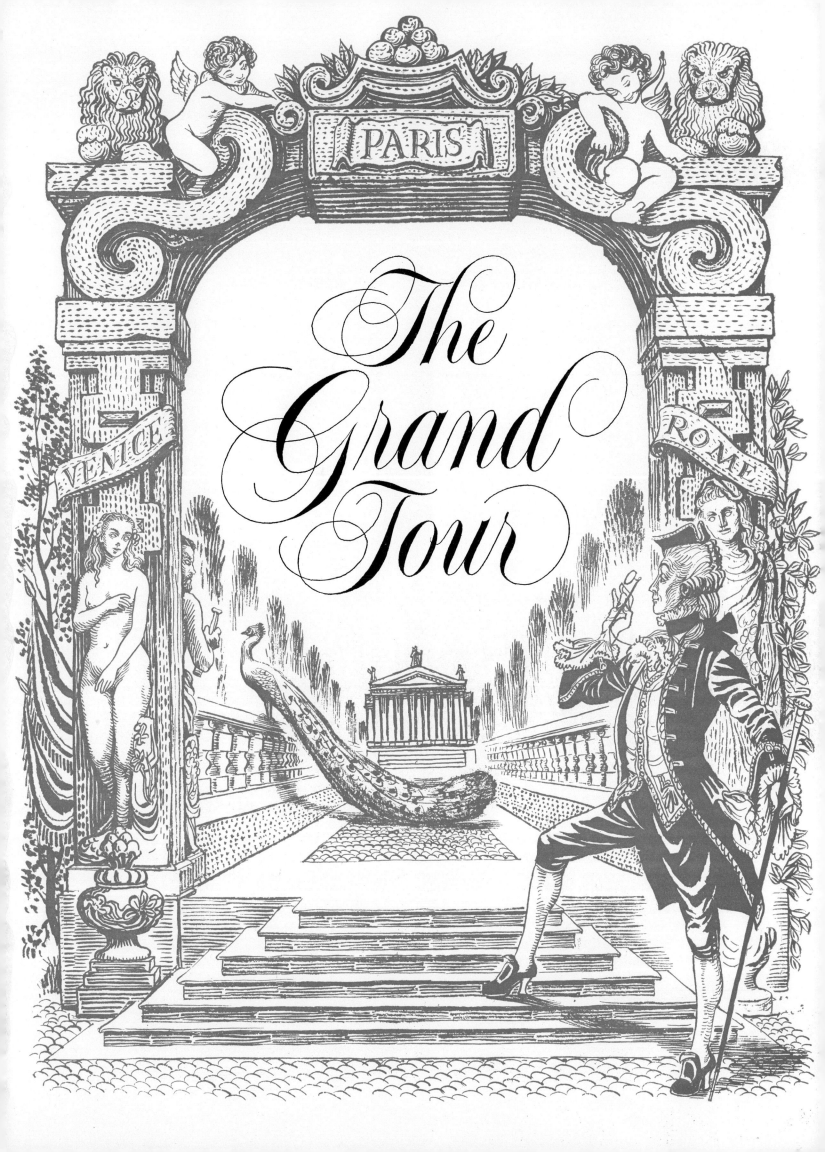

PARIS

VENICE

ROME

The
Grand
Tour

The Grand Tour

It was the most expensive education ever devised. Its classrooms were the capitals of Europe, its textbooks the ruins and monuments of eighteen centuries. From it the young aristocrat could learn, if he chose, how to eat, dress, dance, converse, fight, and make love

By J. H. PLUMB

Before the end of the seventeenth century, education in England, as elsewhere in Europe, was confined to a narrow compass. At a very tender age gentlemen's sons were boarded out with a country parson to learn their letters, their numbers, and the rudiments of Latin grammar—like Robert Walpole, the future Prime Minister of England, who was sent away from home at the age of four. Holidays were sparse—a few days at Christmas and a month at harvest time. At nine or ten the children left the vicarage for the grammar school in the neighboring county town where they boarded with the master. There they rubbed shoulders with local tradesmen's sons. They dressed alike and spoke the same dialect; in those days a difference in social rank did not inhibit close social intercourse. At adolescence their ways tended to part: the shopkeeper's son went to his apprenticeship, the gentleman's son left for the university or the Inns of Court to acquire that extra knowledge of religion and law

that his station required. After two or three years at Oxford and Cambridge (and if his home were distant, there he stayed without a holiday), he returned to help his father with his estate. Apart from a rare visit to London and a more frequent one to the local metropolis—York, Bristol, Norwich, Exeter —his traveling days were over. He lived and died in his neighborhood. And this, with few variations, was the pattern of education throughout northwestern Europe; it differed only for a few aristocrats attached to courts. Sir Philip Sidney was granted a passport to complete his education abroad, to perfect his languages, and to familiarize himself with different nations and governments so that he might be trained to play a part in the affairs of state. Sometimes a likely youth, noticed by a statesman, would be sent to a foreign university to be trained for a career in public administration. But generally governments regarded foreign travel as dangerous: Protestant states feared the wiles of Romish priests might corrupt their young, Catholic ones dreaded the contact with heresy.

By 1700 all this had changed. The grammar schools and universities were no longer crowded with gentlemen's sons; indeed they were emptying fast (Christ's College, Cambridge, had only three freshmen in 1733, and many of its rooms were

The climax of the Tour came in Rome, where the traveler reflected on past glories in the Forum (detail painted by Canaletto) and sought out present-day diversions in the salons.

Gentleman's Pocket Magazine and Album, LONDON 1845

Radio Times HULTON PICTURE LIBRARY

The great adventure began by taking the packet across the heaving English Channel—and wishing one had stayed home.

At Calais a carriage was hired for the trip to Paris, but an underfed horse might not make it to the next posting station.

deserted). Shopkeepers preferred the new education provided by private enterprise, the schools and academies which taught bookkeeping, languages, geography, navigation—the arts necessary for commercial life; gentlemen sent their sons abroad on a Grand Tour. By 1720, no Englishman or German pretending to a place in society could expect to be regarded as anything but a country bumpkin unless he had spent two or three years in France or Italy. The aristocracy of Scandinavia and Russia quickly followed suit. The effect was to give a remarkable homogeneity of manners and taste to the nobility of eighteenth-century Europe.

The reasons for this change are clear and simple. The ferocity of religious conflict had been assuaged by the growing sophistication of the educated classes. True, barbarities were still perpetuated in the name of God. States, however, had grown confident of their abilities to impose the religion of their choice upon their subjects, and the seventeenth century witnessed an ending of religious strife which was also civil. The disruptive powers of religion were no longer acute. The spread of philosophy, the cult of a rational deity and rational universe which became fashionable amongst the upper classes at the same time, made parents fear less the dangers their sons' souls might encounter from a sojourn abroad. Furthermore, northwestern Europe was growing rich on the fat commercial profits which the New Worlds, East and West, had brought into being. Sugar, tobacco, slaves, and spices made the guineas jingle in the pockets of nobleman and merchant from Bristol to Hamburg. Rich, they were also raw. Italians, and even Frenchmen, were aware of their magnifi-

cent heritage from the ancient world. Buildings of beauty still greeted them either in decay or in ruin. Scientists, philosophers, historians, poets all proclaimed the greatness of *their* past. But the English, the Germans, the Russians, the Scandinavians possessed no ancient glory. A broken military wall, an arch here and there merely proclaimed their ancient slavery to Rome. Apart from these, they possessed only what their age professed to regard as barbarous—the great Gothic cathedrals and the vast castles of their immediate feudal past. Their nations had grown up outside the pale of culture; they belonged to Europe's remoter provinces, to its frontiers with the outer world. They knew themselves to be uncouth. And this had been made even more self-evident to them by the splendors of the court of Louis XIV.

At Versailles Louis had created a world of sophisticated, aristocratic grandeur. His palace was vaster than any that had been built since the days of Imperial Rome. His painters and his poets constantly harked back in their pictures and their dramas to the glories of the Roman Empire, hinting that in Louis and in France, Europe had at last found an equal to the magnificence of Augustus and his age. The classical world, either in its reflection in the Italian Renaissance or in its own right, entranced Europe. No gentleman worthy of the name could be unfamiliar with the writers of antiquity, and Latin tags were bandied about in the House of Commons, the Virginia Assembly, and the Polish Diet. And throughout Europe developed the feeling that at last the long centuries of barbarism were over, and that life could be lived with that elegance combined with dignity which was the hall-

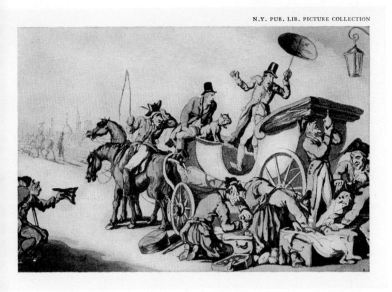

The unwritten law at French customhouses: repack your own bags or bribe the willing douaniers—discreetly, of course.

When night fell the traveler entered a French inn grimly wondering if he could survive the cooking and the bedding.

mark of Roman gentility. Louis XIV had achieved far more than a mere imitation of imperial grandeur. He had developed the arts of war and diplomacy to an efficiency which no other kingdom could rival, although all desired to do so. Soldiers and ambassadors in embryo could learn their trades only in France. And it was the only place where a nobleman could learn to live according to his station; there he could discover how an aristocrat should eat, dress, dance, converse, love, and fight. Yet France itself was not sufficient: taste could be properly formed only by a visit to the fountainhead of antiquity itself—Italy. Some even considered Italy superior to France in teaching the young nobleman how to make love.

To learn manners, to learn the only trades open to an aristocrat—war and diplomacy—to learn the culture of his class made a Grand Tour a necessity for the young English or German peer. Fortunately the new wealth that was seeping into Europe enabled him to afford what was the most extravagant form of education ever devised by European society. The young nobleman resided abroad usually for three, but often for four, and at times even five years. More often than not he was accompanied by two tutors: one for bookish study, the other for riding, fencing, the arts of war. Often the former were men of distinction—Adam Smith, the economist, accompanied the Duke of Buccleuch; William Coxe, the historian, tutored Lord Herbert. Usually one personal servant was taken from England, the others hired as necessary. The grandest people shipped their own coaches, but the enterprising hotelier, Monsieur Dessin of Calais, ran a highly profitable coach-hire business and had a virtual monopoly on it.

Usually the Tour started very modestly with a stay in a French provincial town, preferably where the English were few, so that the boy was forced to speak French. Strasbourg, Dijon, Lyons were favored because they afforded convenient places for short tours to Germany and Switzerland. Others preferred the towns in the Touraine because the purest French was spoken there. A boy's day was meticulously regulated. William Coxe was instructed to make "a return of the occupations of every day in the week and at what hours" to the Earl of Pembroke. Both Coxe and Captain Floyd, young Lord Herbert's second tutor, and the boy himself had to give an account of themselves on the first, tenth, and twentieth of every month. The young man's hours of riding, fencing, dancing, tennis, and billiards were as keenly regulated as his mathematics, history, and geography. He was ordered to a dentist twice a year, commanded to take a purge of camomile tea every morning before eating, and to have the tips of his hair trimmed on the second day of every new moon. This vigorous, almost remorseless system could be kept up only whilst the boy was young, the society in which he moved alien and strange, and the tutors still in awe of the noble father at home. Paris with its salons and sophistication usually proved irresistible and the tutors' resistance easily overcome.

Paris either entranced or disappointed; the incurable Anglophiles saw it as a meaner, shabbier London, but the majority were delighted by the clean streets, brilliant lighting, and the lovely royal gardens designed by Le Nôtre; gardens made for elegant lounging and discreet flirtation. Here the young Englishmen, Germans, and Russians came to gape at

TEXT CONTINUED ON PAGE 86

*F*or the young Englishman who
hoped to perfect his manners as
well as to improve his mind, it was
obligatory to make a side trip to the
court at Versailles. There, twelve
miles outside Paris, he found the
most sumptuous palace in the world
—created by Louis XIV out of his
father's hunting lodge, and maintained by his successors in profligate splendor until the Revolution. In 1668, when Pierre Patel
painted this view, one could still
identify the original lodge as the
square center portion. But great
changes had been made: annexes,
parterres, gardens, a vast new park,
and the mile-long Grand Canal had
already turned it into an opulent
setting for the King, arriving in a
scarlet coach to the blare of trum-
pets and the thunder of drums. In
the next century, Englishmen on
the Grand Tour tended to view all
this pomp as a vulgar extravagance.

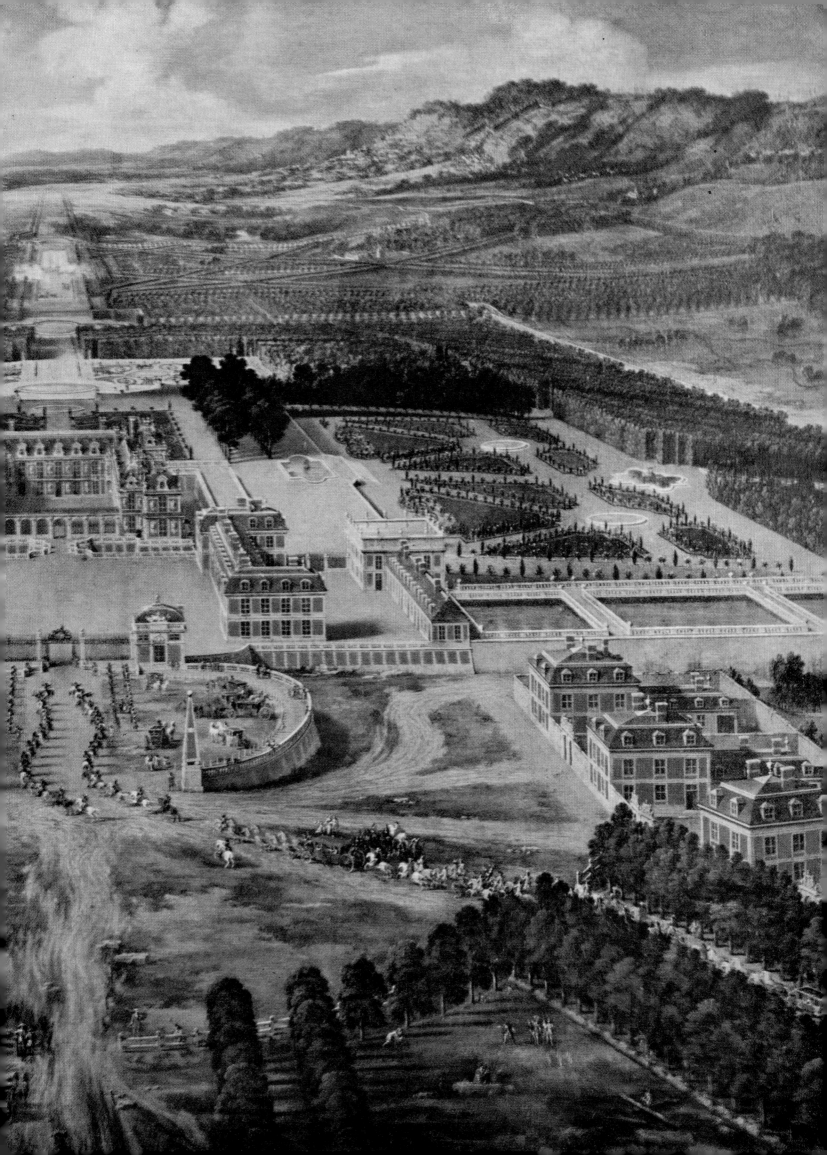

A few moments spent with Voltaire at Ferney, near Geneva, was the goal of all those who considered him the greatest mind in Europe. He received visitors so freely that during the Seven Years' War he was embarrassed when rival Russians, Englishmen, and Germans confronted each other in his rooms. He wore a blue and gold satin robe and nightcap even while counseling kings and statesmen from his bed.

The most brilliant salon of the day was that of Mme Geoffrin (above), who ruled supreme in her little "kingdom on the Rue Saint-Honoré." The wealthy hostess in her famous lace bonnet (right foreground) invited noblemen and scholars from all over Europe to her international social club. In this painting by Lemonnier, the actor Le Kain reads to an assembly that includes such great names as Jean-Jacques Rousseau and the Encyclopedists Diderot and d'Alembert. Only taboo: politics.

To see fashionable Paris on parade one went to the gardens of the Palais-Royal (left), where gentlemen met cocottes and actresses from the adjoining theater (now the Comédie Française). This was still going on—although with some lowering of tone—in the nineteenth century, after Debucourt made this painting of dandies who are giving a perilous tilt to their chairs to impress the ladies. The gay dog at the right, who turns with a flourish to throw a kiss, is none other than the future king, Louis-Philippe.

OVERLEAF: Among the glories of Paris which every Grand Tourist had to see was the stained glass of Sainte-Chapelle, built in the thirteenth century to house the relics of the Crown of Thorns and a bit of the True Cross. The great pageant depicted here took place in 1715 when the young Louis XV was taken to the chapel before confirming the regency of the Duke of Orleans. The boy king, a tiny figure in white, is being carried under the wide center arch.

THE ENGLISHMAN ON HIS ADVENTURES ABROAD

Far removed from the melancholy of his Elegy in a Country Churchyard, *the poet Thomas Gray writes his mother of an evening in 1739 in Rheims:*

The other evening we happened to be got together in a company of eighteen people, men and women of the best fashion here, at a garden in the town to walk; when one of the ladies bethought herself of asking, 'Why should we not sup here?' Immediately the cloth was laid by the side of the fountain under the trees, and a very elegant supper served up; after which another said, 'Come, let us sing'; and directly began herself. From singing we insensibly fell to dancing, and singing in the round; when somebody mentioned violins; and immediately a company of them was ordered. Minuets were begun in the open air, and then came country dances, which held till four o'clock next morning, at which hour the gayest lady there proposed that such as were weary should get into their coaches, and the rest of them should dance before them, with the music in the van; and in this manner we paraded through all the principal streets of the city, and waked everybody in it.

The sportsman Peter Beckford writes to an English friend about foreign language problems in 1785:

As in our language we are not embarrassed with articles, we see no reason why a knife should be masculine, and a fork feminine; and still less, why a coach should be of one gender in France and another in Italy; and yet, discreet as we usually are in the use of our genders, in one instance we are as bad as our neighbors, when we make a female of a man-of-war. This is the most difficult part of every language, and when we English begin to speak French or Italian is the cause of many laughable mistakes, and sometimes of indecent ones. Bad pronunciation also, for which we are famous, often occasions an equivoque. The Englishman who said, *"J'ai été un âne à Paris et je serai un âne à Rome,"* was believed, though it was plainly perceived he did not mean what he said.

The novelist Tobias Smollett describes the foibles of his countrymen on the Continent:

They are supposed to have more money to throw away; and therefore a greater number of snares are layed for them. This opinion of their superior wealth they take a pride in confirming by launching out into all manner of unnecessary expense, but what is still more dangerous, the moment they set foot in Italy they are seized with the ambition of becoming connoisseurs in painting, music, statuary, and architecture; and the adventurers of this country don't fail to flatter this weakness for their own advantage. I have seen in different parts of Italy a number of raw boys, whom Britain seemed to have poured forth on pur-

pose to bring her national character into contempt; ignorant, petulant, rash, and profligate, without any knowledge or experience of their own, without any director to improve their understanding, or superintend their conduct. One engages in play with an infamous gamester, and is stripped perhaps in the very first partie; another is poxed and pillaged by an antiquated cantatrice; a third is bubbled by a knavish antiquarian, and a fourth is led in contribution by a dealer in pictures. Some turn fiddlers, and pretend to compose, but all of them talk familiarly of the arts and return finished connoisseurs and coxcombs, to their own country. The most remarkable phenomenon of this kind, which I have seen, is a boy of 72, now actually traveling through Italy, for improvement, under the auspices of another boy of 22.

Seasoned by travel, Edward Gibbon in 1789 offers advice to others:

I will briefly describe the qualifications which I deem most essential to a traveler. He should be endowed with an active, indefatigable vigor of mind and body, which can seize every mode of conveyance, and support, with a careless smile, every hardship of the road, the weather, or the inn. It must stimulate him with a restless curiosity, impatient of ease, covetous of time, and fearless of dangers; which drives him forth, at any hour of the day or night, to drive the flood, to climb the mountain, or to fathom the mine on the most doubtful promise of entertainment and instruction. The arts of common life are not studied in the closet; with a copious stock of classical and historical learning, my traveler must blend the practical knowledge of husbandry and manufactures; he should be a chymist, a botanist, and a master of mechanics. A musical ear will multiply the pleasures of his Italian tour; but a correct and exquisite eye, which commands the landskip of a country, discerns the merit of a picture, and measures the proportions of a building, is more closely connected with the finer feelings of the mind, and the fleeting image shall be fixed and realized by the dexterity of the pencil.

I have reserved for the last a virtue which borders on a vice; the flexible temper which can assimilate itself to every tone of society from the court to the cottage; the happy flow of spirits which can amuse and be amused in every company and situation. With the advantage of an independent fortune and the ready use of national and provincial idioms, the traveler should unite the pleasing aspect and decent familiarity which makes every stranger an acquaintance, and the art of conversing with ignorance and dullness on some topic of local or professional information. The benefits of foreign travel will correspond with the degrees of these various qualifications.

ℰvery true British traveler yearned for one golden moment above and beyond the worthy sensations promised by his guidebook. Perhaps he saw it as a Fragonard canvas come to life, a Fête at Rambouillet (below) where he, too, feasted amidst the cascades and rose bowers, listened to tinkling music, and enjoyed the nearness of beautiful ladies. In a letter opposite, the poet Thomas Gray shows that such dreams came true.

En route again: the Alps go by in a blur as the diligence tears down through St. Gotthard pass.

A calmer way to see nature was the newly popular sport of mountain-climbing in Switzerland.

TEXT CONTINUED FROM PAGE 77

fashion and to grow accustomed to the new French clothes it was *de rigueur* to buy on arrival in Paris. Even Dr. Johnson, who made his Grand Tour very late in life, gave up his brown fustian and went into silk and lace the day he arrived. Naturally the wellborn were amply provided with introductions to aristocratic circles and usually they were presented at Court. Weeks of balls and parties followed, interspersed with sightseeing and buying luxurious gewgaws—gold snuffboxes, seals of carnelian and agate, the lovely porcelain of Sèvres; fine velvets, silks, and damasks; screens, fans, *étuis,* clocks in ormolu and marble; watches framed in diamonds; daring terra cottas by Clodion and bronzes by Bouchardon. All were boxed, packed, insured, and dispatched against the day when the exile returned to his distant province. Before Paris endangered the morals or ruined the finances, the young nobleman's steps would be diverted towards Italy. Until 1780, the usual routes were either through Savoy and over the Mont Cenis to Turin or by boat down the Rhone and by felucca— a coastal sailing craft—from Antibes to Genoa. Both could be exciting. The Mont Cenis route necessitated taking the coach to pieces and carrying the traveler in a chair over the steepest part of the path, a formidable undertaking in winter when bad weather might endanger everyone's life. During his passage, Horace Walpole had his favorite lap dog seized from under his nose by a wolf. The danger of the other route lay in the treacherous nature of the swift-flowing Rhone, particularly at Pont-Saint-Esprit, and after that there was always the possibility that the felucca would be seized by the Barbary corsairs that roamed the Mediterranean: rich Christians

fetched a good ransom. After 1750, however, mountains became fashionable and the sea route grew neglected. The marvels of nature—particularly glaciers and above all the *Mer de Glace* on Mont Blanc—began to be admired and no Grand Tour was complete without a mountaineering adventure. So, on the way to Italy, many stopped off at Chamonix. Armed with guides and loaded with barometers, tea kettles to boil water on the glacier and so determine heights, luncheon baskets, tents, and servants (the Empress Josephine took sixty-eight guides in 1810!) they braved the mountainside. Sometimes even an artist was hired to render the scene immortal—Lord Palmerston took a famous water-colorist, William Pars; so did Beckford, who had with him J. R. Cozens. Their drawings are some of the earliest we have of romantically viewed mountain scenery. Amidst the towering peaks of snow and ice all felt a proper sense of fear, of man's insignificance, of the majesty and indifference of Nature. More than twenty years after his visit, Dr. Howard of Baltimore, one of the early travelers to the *Mer de Glace,* said: "I cannot even now think of some of the situations without a feeling of dread." Earlier generations, like that of Addison and afterwards of Gibbon, had ignored these mountains and concentrated on a course of comparative constitutional study for which the multiplicity of states and cities in Switzerland provided ample material. But it was of the nature of the Grand Tour to increase in entertainment and diminish in education as time passed; also romanticism, through Rousseau, was making the transition easier by insisting that the feelings needed education as much as the mind.

Most relaxing of all was sight-seeing in Venice, where one paid the gondolier to do all the work.

The tourist jogged over volcanic ash in a chair-lift to peer into the crater of Mount Vesuvius.

Italy was, perhaps, the most important part of any tour and a far longer time was usually spent in it. As Dr. Johnson said: "A man who has not been in Italy is always conscious of an inferiority."

Italy was the land of marvels, the antique shop of Europe. Speculators dug feverishly for Roman marbles and bronzes, and the discoveries at Herculaneum and Pompeii inflamed the imagination still further. All Englishmen were expected to return festooned with works of art and they became dilettantes overnight, talking with assurance of patina and of significant form. They ransacked palaces, abbeys, and convents, employed spies and informers, and were easily, too easily, gulled by fakes. But throughout the century an ever-increasing stream of works of art—good, bad, and indifferent— flowed into the country houses of England, Germany, Scandinavia, and Russia. Italy, however, offered more than art. "Indeed," pontificated Dr. Johnson, "if a young man is wild, and must run after women and bad company, it is better this should be done abroad, as, on his return, he can break off such connections and begin at home a new man." Better an Italian countess, Catholic and married, than an English actress, marriageable but impossible. Furthermore the Italian countess was likely to improve his style not only in the arts of elegant flirtation but also in training him for the marriage bed. And the worldly-wise parents expected their young to lose their hearts in Italy; some like Lord Pembroke recommended their old flames to their sons and wrote sentimentally about their own past. Strenuous sight-seeing days followed by nights, equally strenuous, of amorous dalliance completed the

education of the young nobleman abroad. But it was a leisurely finish—Turin, Milan, Rome (the Jacobite Court carefully avoided), Naples for the ruins and the opera, and then Verona for Palladio's sake, and Venice for its Carnival. The pictures of Longhi—suggestive, raffish, elegant—recall for us the dissolute nature of Venice's charm. Here the mask permitted license.

After one or two years in Italy, the long voyage home began. The traveler had left England as a stripling unversed in the arts of life; he returned sophisticated, urbane, and a *cognoscente*. His portrait painted by Batoni, Rosalba, or Mengs; one or two pictures of the first rank, sometimes genuine, sometimes false; a collection of water colors, drawings, and lithographs; the latest volumes on Pompeii from the royal press of Naples; marbles, bronzes, Genoa velvet, and Capodimonte porcelain that would embellish his state rooms were packed in their great crates and sent home via a warship for safety's sake. On his return to Paris, the success of his Grand Tour could be measured by the ease with which he bore himself in the salons. Back at home, he joined a magic circle. By

TEXT CONTINUED ON PAGE 90

OVERLEAF: The height of the social season in Venice was the annual Ascension Day ceremony in May, Guardi's De-parture of the Bucentaur shows the doge leaving in his richly decorated craft for the Lido, where he dropped a ring in the Adriatic and proclaimed, "I wed thee, sea." Venetians were thus reminded that they owed everything to the sea, and that their unique position on it had made them rich.

87

TEXT CONTINUED FROM PAGE 87

turning the conversation to stories of Madame du Deffand, or by the mention of a picture in the Pitti, or the prices charged by Busiri, he could quickly get the measure of each new acquaintance and discover whether he belonged to his own aristocratic world. This prolonged, extravagant education was achieved only at great cost—a young nobleman abroad could easily run his father into three or four thousand pounds a year (by modern standards some sixty thousand dollars a year). Expensive though it might be, it drew more and more people into its orbit; indeed, not only the young and aristocratic but also the middle-aged and the middle class.

The fascination of a European tour even began to intrigue the well-to-do in the American States and the West Indies. By the end of the century, English, Germans, Scandinavians, bourgeois as well as aristocrats, began to swarm to the warm south. Philip Thicknesse pioneered and popularized the idea of making the Grand Tour cheaply. In 1790 William Wordsworth, the poet, and his friend Robert Jones were perhaps the first undergraduates to make the tour on foot with their belongings strapped to their backs. As steamships and railways replaced the sailing ship and the coach, the swarm became a flood and finally submerged the Grand Tour. Under the pressure of middle-class values, aristocratic standards of education began to give way and the tutor and the Grand Tour were replaced by the public school and university. Entertainment became the aim of foreign travel rather than education and fine manners.

During its heyday, however, the Grand Tour had influenced social life to a remarkable degree; it also created the basic structure of foreign travel which later generations were to adopt and to extend. Some

of the diaries and journals, which all travelers tended to keep, got into print; others stayed in the family archives to warn and exhort and advise youngsters. As the eighteenth century progressed, descriptive literature gave way to practical guides. Thomas Taylor's *The Gentleman's Pocket Companion for Traveling into Foreign Parts,* which provided maps, advised on roads, and gave distances, also printed tables of money and weights for conversion, listed a huge variety of information, and gave as well simple dialogues in Italian, French, German, and Spanish. It quickly became every traveler's *vade mecum* and spawned a vast brood of guides that have never ceased to pour from publishing houses.

Nor were the journalists, publishers, amateur writers the only men to see that money was to be made out of the passion for the Grand Tour. Fencing masters, dancing masters, riding masters did so excellent a trade in Paris that their professions became overcrowded. The least successful drifted to Moscow, Budapest, Edinburgh, and Stockholm to take the education in manners to the *petite bourgeoisie* who could not afford either the time or the money to leave their native heath, but wanted their sons and daughters to ape the airs of the aristocracy. Language masters often pioneered the way, for it became a mark of gentility in all countries to be able to interlard conversation with a few phrases in Italian or French. Although moralists might denounce the corruption of native manners that French and Italian airs always produced, there can be little doubt that the rage for southern European culture softened the barbarity and increased the civility of countries in the west, north, and east of Europe. Yet when carried to excess, as it was in some German courts

TEXT CONTINUED ON PAGE 94

PORTRAIT FROM "THE DUNCIAD"

Alexander Pope in his *Dunciad* (1728) drew a classic portrait of the young Englishman on tour. Returning from his year abroad, the traveler is presented to the Goddess of Dulness in these words:

"Thro' School and College, thy kind cloud o'ercast,
Safe and unseen the young Aeneas past:
Thence bursting glorious, all at once let down,
Stunn'd with his giddy Larum half the town.
Intrepid then, o'er seas and lands he flew:
Europe he saw, and Europe saw him too.
There all thy gifts and graces we display,
Thou, only thou, directing all our way!
To where the Seine, obsequious as she runs,
Pours at great Bourbon's feet her silken sons;
Or Tiber, now no longer Roman, rolls,
Vain of Italian arts, Italian souls:
To happy Convents, bosom'd deep in vines,
Where slumber Abbots, purple as their wines;
To Isles of fragrance, lily-silver'd vales,
Diffusing languor in the panting gales:
To lands of singing, or of dancing slaves,
Love-whisp'ring woods, and lute-resounding waves.
But chief her shrine where naked Venus keeps,
And Cupids ride the Lion of the Deeps;
Where, eas'd of Fleets, the Adriatic main
Wafts the smooth Eunuch and enamour'd swain.
Led by my hand, he saunter'd Europe round,
And gather'd ev'ry Vice on Christian ground;
Saw ev'ry Court, heard ev'ry King declare
His royal sense of Op'ras or the Fair:
The Stews and Palace equally explor'd
Intrigu'd with glory and with spirit w——;
Try'd all hors d'œuvres, all liqueurs defin'd,
Judicious drank, and greatly daring din'd;
Dropt the dull lumber of the Latin store,
Spoil'd his own language and acquir'd no more;
All Classic learning lost on Classic ground,
And last turn'd Air, the Echo of a Sound!
See now, half-cur'd and perfectly well-bred,
With nothing but a Solo in his head."

90

A cultural mecca for English visitors to Florence was the Tribuna of the Uffizi Gallery (at right)—a rendezvous commemorated by the fashionable eighteenth-century painter Zoffany, whose swarming canvases made him a favorite of the British royal family. It was they, in fact, who commissioned this picture—and asked that it include the gallery, the paintings and sculpture, and some of their wandering nationals. Among the works of art are the Venus de Medici on the pedestal at the right, Titian's Reclining Venus in the foreground, and two Raphael Madonnas at left. At right, with sword and decoration, is the English envoy to Florence, Sir Horace Mann. Zoffany himself is shown holding one of the Raphaels at the left—perhaps to give a lecture on color and composition.

His travels as a tutor allowed Adam Smith (left) to exchange ideas with French philosophers and develop the theories he put in his Wealth of Nations. *But gaiety, not profound thinking, was the goal of all who called on the British ambassador at Naples, Sir William Hamilton (right) and his wife Emma. The fascinating Emma (later Lord Nelson's mistress) delighted guests with her Grecian "attitudes," and was painted as the Muse of Comedy (opposite).*

TEXT CONTINUED FROM PAGE 90

and amongst the aristocracy of Russia, it possessed dangers. The noblemen of Russia spoke French, dressed in French clothes, sat on French furniture, mostly employed French servants, and became alien to their own people and their problems; and the cleavage between classes in Russia was immeasurably widened. In Germany the nationalistically minded *bourgeoisie* turned under the influence of the *Aufklärung* from emulation to envy and hate, and cultivated Teutonic customs—crude, absurd, cloudy with bourgeois romance—as a sort of protest against the aristocratic attitude of international culture derived from Greece and Rome and kept alive in France and Italy, of which the Grand Tour was the symbol. Perhaps both these disruptive effects were natural responses to the greatest achievement of the Grand Tour. This was to give a homogeneity of attitude to the European aristocracy, a homogeneity never achieved since by any class on such an international scale: James Boswell had no difficulty in slipping into the best aristocratic society in Utrecht, Berlin, Darmstadt, Geneva, Florence, Venice, Milan, Naples, Paris; yet he was, as Scottish gentlemen went, rather a raw youth of no great family distinction. Horace Walpole, a youth of twenty, fitted into the highest circles in France and Italy with instinctive ease: taste, knowledge, background, and education were the same—whatever their race —for young men of his birth and breeding. Their early years had been spent in learning those arts of living which the Grand Tour brought to perfection. It made for ease not

only in the transmission of taste but also of ideas. Voltaire, Rousseau, Diderot, Gibbon, Hume were read about as quickly in St. Petersburg or Naples as in their native lands. Yet the Grand Tour probably had its most profound effect in two spheres—travel and taste.

The rudimentary foundation upon which the huge structure of modern European travel has been erected came into being very largely to fulfill the needs of the young aristocrats setting out on their tours. Hotels, couriers, foreign exchange facilities, specialized transport to beauty spots—the whole paraphernalia by which the aristocrats were transported, housed, fed, and informed came into being in eighteenth-century Europe. By and large these early travelers found and fixed upon what were to become the playgrounds of Europe. They discovered the delights of the Alps and made Switzerland a tourist center of Europe; they recommended the French and Italian Rivieras for their climate and their cheapness. Before the end of the century the old and delicate from northern Europe were infesting Nice, Menton, and San Remo; the unmarried aunts of the European peerage drifted into the resorts—throughout France and Italy—which their noble ancestors had discovered on their Grand Tours.

Yet the greatest influence of the Grand Tour was in art and taste. Every museum in northern Europe owes something to the wealth and skill of those young aristocrats who made the Grand Tour, and bought on the strength of their taste— or rather the taste of that small band of Anglo-Roman ex-

The glum self-portrait of Joshua Reynolds, at right, was probably painted after a mishap in Minorca, which he described in 1749: "I have been kept here near two months by an odd accident—a fall from a horse down a precipice, which cut my face in such a manner as confined me to my room. The unlucky part of the question is my lips are spoiled for kissing and the rest so disfigured that I have but a sorry face to look at." For a gay bachelor, this was misfortune indeed.

patriates who devoted themselves to the British nobility's passion for sight-seeing and for art. Usually they were failed architects or artists like Colin Morrison, James Byres, and John Parker. They usually could be found hanging about the English coffeehouse in the Piazza di Spagna, waiting for their custom. They gave good value. James Byres took the historian Edward Gibbon on a tour of Roman antiquities that lasted eighteen weeks without a day's intermission, and left Gibbon exhausted. Even the indefatigable Boswell, who in a fit of enthusiasm insisted that he and Morrison speak Latin as they visited the Forum, discovered that he lacked the stamina and the spirit to maintain a passionate interest as Morrison remorselessly plodded in the Roman heat up and down the hills and in and out of the ruins, leaving nothing undescribed. Usually these *cicerones*, as they were called, kept a close contact with Italian painters and art dealers, collecting a double commission from the patron and the patronized. Byres was responsible for the Portland Vase reaching England, and the sale of Poussin's *Seven Sacraments* was also negotiated by him. Obviously the young noblemen felt much safer if buying through one of their own countrymen: a weakness which a shrewd Welshman, Thomas Jenkins, turned to his own great profit. He became the leading art dealer in Rome. Often the aristocrat could not raise the huge sums Jenkins demanded for his statues, so he lent the money for the purchase and thus took a double profit. Jenkins's histrionic powers were highly developed: he wept with emotion at parting with an object on

which he was making several thousand per cent profit. His head, however, was equal to his heart and no one could match him in the technique of restoration; under his skillful hands a battered antique torso quickly achieved arms, legs, and head with the finest nicotine staining to give them an age worthy of the price that he charged. Nor was he humble to his clients. He underlined their ignorance, paraded his own virtuosity, and plucked their pockets in the mood of humility so induced. And, of course, there were far less reputable sharks than Jenkins, eager to catch the gullible nobleman with a bargain at an exorbitant price. The standards of professional honesty were low and the skill in copying old masters high, and many a Raphael was born to blush when seen in the cold, critical, northern light.

No traveler came back empty-handed: pictures, statuary, and bronzes, ranging from antique Greek marbles to water colors by fashionable Italians, were brought back in thousands to enable English, Dutch, Germans, Russians, and Scandinavians to appreciate and enjoy the great aristocratic inheritance of Europe. The astonishing virtuosity of these young men can be seen from a recent exhibition held at Norwich which displayed works collected on the Grand Tour during the eighteenth century, principally by the leading Norfolk families. This not only contained old masters, but also illustrated the patronage they brought to eighteenth-century Italian artists. No Italian artist of real merit was absent and the quality of many of their works was exceptional;

there were magnificent examples of Canaletto, Guardi, Piranesi, Zuccarelli, Batoni, Rosalba, Pannini, Busiri, the Riccis.

This passion for all things Italianate, whether antique or modern, forced painters and architects to make their own pilgrimages to Rome, for they stood little chance of making a living in England unless they could parade a recognizable virtuosity to the returned tourists. So off they went: some, like Reynolds, by man-of-war in the luxury of great patronage; others, like Thomas Patch, on foot in poverty. They reached Italy in droves; some died there, some stayed, most returned with improved techniques and many splendid canvases to stimulate the powers and imagination of those who stayed at home. Strangely few Italian artists attempted to exploit the English market in its homeland; the most outstanding of these was Canaletto whose pictures of London, Windsor, and Alnwick Castle are amongst the finest topographical paintings of the eighteenth-century English scene.

Passionately preoccupied as tourists were with art, few developed a keen critical judgment or displayed much independence of mind. They were willing to pay huge prices for Veroneses and Titians, they prized Caravaggios and eagerly bought early Bolognese painters—Guido Reni, Guercino, and the Caraccis—artists who are now regarded as far, far inferior to Tintoretto or Botticelli whom they consistently ignored. As in painting, so in architecture: they confined themselves strictly to the limits of the fashionable, thought St. Mark's at Venice barbarous, and kept their praise for Caserta by Vanvitelli or for Bernini's colonnades at St. Peter's. Their classical education, however, gave them a profound interest in the discoveries at Pompeii and Herculaneum. Sir William Hamilton with his lovely wife Emma, afterwards Nelson's mistress, acted as host to a whole generation of the British aristocracy and not only taught them the beauties of classical design, but often secured objects for them that were both authentic and beautiful. Indeed the pilgrimage to Pompeii strengthened considerably the adoption of classical motives in architecture and decoration which marks the last half of the eighteenth century. The wily Josiah Wedgwood was quick to exploit this acquired taste of returned aristocrats, and he manufactured for them huge quantities of pottery in Pompeian shapes festooned with classical reliefs. Indeed, he called his factory "Etruria."

The ideas, the attitudes, the tastes fostered and extended by the Grand Tour imbued the aristocracy with more than sophistication. They regarded themselves as the true heirs of the Augustans. They came, in consequence, to believe passionately in the virtues of courage and stoicism. They thought nothing became them so well as heroic death in the service of their country, and in the wars against Napoleon they died as well as many a Roman. Furthermore they regarded an interest in classical literature and a capacity to judge the decorative arts as essential qualities of a gentleman. At least these were the standards in which they believed, even though many fell short of them; for all did not respond, as Adam Smith realized, to the educational values of the Grand Tour. He thought that the boy "commonly returns home more conceited, more unprincipled, more dissipated, and more incapable of any serious application, either to study or to business than he could well have become in so short a time had he lived at home." True of some, it was not the common experience. The country houses of England, its museums and galleries, the vast literature of travel, the increased urbanity and the growth of civility of English social life in the late eighteenth century, reflected in the correspondence of Horace Walpole, show that this fabulously extravagant education for a ruling class—more costly than any invented before or enjoyed since—paid fat dividends. The rich are not always remarkable for taste, wit, elegance, but the eighteenth-century aristocracy throughout Europe insisted on these virtues. Thanks to the Grand Tour, taste acquired in Italy, combined with the breeding acquired in France, brought sophistication to the remoter outposts of European society which had previously lived close to barbarism. It also gave to the Western world a love of ancient Europe and its artistic heritage that has long ceased to be confined to the aristocracy. What was once the unique privilege of a nobleman is now the common experience of the English-speaking peoples.

J. H. Plumb is a Fellow of Christ's College, Cambridge, and an outstanding authority on the eighteenth century. He is co-author of The American Heritage Book of the Revolution.

I could have cried with pleasure," exclaimed a visitor upon viewing Saint Peter's in Rome. "Sublime" was the word most often used to describe the exterior, but many tourists were disappointed with their first view of the interior. Only after walking about the marbled floor and standing beneath the soaring arches and airy dome did they appreciate "that vastness which grows, but grows to harmonize"—as Lord Byron put it. Pannini's painting illustrates the accuracy of Byron's observation.

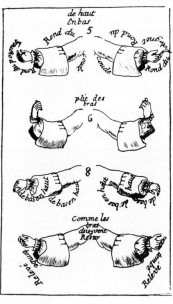

POSITIONS, ARM MOVEMENTS, AND FLOOR PATTERN OF THE MINUET FROM *Le Maître à Danser*, PIERRE RAMEAU, PARIS 1734; FLOOR PATTERN OF THE COQUETTE FROM *Recueil de Contredanses Fransois et Anglois*, RAOUL FEUILLET, PARIS 1716

A CURRICULUM FOR GENTLEMEN

The School of Fencing, DOMENICO ANGELO, LONDON 1765

Croupade, cabriole, ballottade, AND GROUND PATTERNS FROM *L'Art de la Cavalerie*, GASPARD DE SAUNIER, PARIS 1756

98

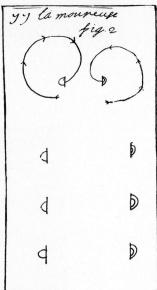

In Paris and Rome the young aristocrats quickly sought out—and made rich—those teachers who specialized in adding "grace to the gifts which nature has bestowed." They went to the dancing masters with their elaborate manuals (above) to learn not only the proper steps but the etiquette of the ballroom—how to doff a hat, maintain a flawless line in gesture and movement, and bow in courtly salute of a lady. The fencing master (left) improved their agility and co-ordination, and taught them such techniques as the use of sword and dagger or cloak and lantern. And though they already knew how to ride, it was on the Continent that they learned the refinements of *haute école* horsemanship (below). Useless for riding to the hounds, it might enable them to cut a dashing figure in the cavalry. They were also expected to learn the arts of love —but for that they found eager instructresses everywhere.

AND THEN CAME THE AMERICANS

ursting with their new independence, Americans were eager to polish their talents in the great classroom of Europe and to enrich their country with the trophies of culture. Washington Irving (right) came to write, and discovered that his subject was not Europe but the rich vein of American folklore he had left behind. A Charleston aristocrat, John Izard Middleton, began by sketching the ruins of Rome—as in his *View from the Summit of Monte Cavo* below—and became one of the first American archaeologists. Middleton often met Irving in the salon of Mme Récamier or of Mme de Staël, who thought Americans "the avant-garde of the human race." Henry Wadsworth Longfellow left New England in the 1820's and again in the 1830's to improve his knowledge of European languages—and returned to write his sagas of America. In 1868 the poet, aged and famous, was back in Rome with his daughter Edith and was painted beneath the Arch of Titus (opposite). This curious picture is the work of three different American artists, who included their own portraits in the foreground. Frederick Church, sitting, painted the arch; Jervis McEntee, in the middle, threw in the view of the Colosseum; and G. P. A. Healy, at right, did all of the figures.

PALACE OF CHARLOTTENBURG, BERLIN

GRADUATION DAY
FOR THE TOURIST

*A*n orgy of spending marked the end of the Grand Tour when paintings and statuary by the ton were sent home as souvenirs. Having one's portrait painted abroad was essential, and canvases such as the one being crated in Watteau's *Sign of Gersaint* (detail above) would soon hang on the walls of the family mansion. The avid collector Charles Towneley bought everything in sight when the contents of Hadrian's villa were dispersed, and then celebrated the feat by having the painter Zoffany cram the entire collection into a single canvas (opposite). These marbles and terra cottas later enriched the British Museum. But like any other form of education, the Grand Tour had its lamentable failures. While some young men collected art, others merely picked up habits— and came home in a state that left their parents aghast (following page). They were now ready for membership in London's "Macaroni Club," but little else.

The Grand Tour, R. S. LAMBERT, FABER 1935

'Welladay! Is This My Son Tom?'

An eighteenth-century father greets his son, returning from the Grand Tour

By ADA LOUISE HUXTABLE

STREET FURNITURE

COMMONPLACE OUTDOOR OBJECTS
FROM LAMPS TO BENCHES AND
KIOSKS OFFER OPPORTUNITIES
FOR GOOD, BAD, OR NO DESIGN
AND SERVE TO MARK A CITY'S
STYLE OR THE ABSENCE OF IT

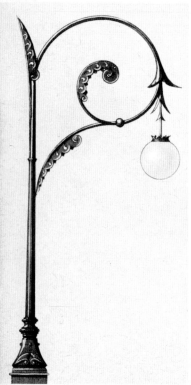

NEW YORK CITY, 1870'S   BOSTON, EARLY 19TH C.   NEW YORK CITY, 1870'S   NEW YORK CITY, TODAY   STATE

The stamp of a city's personality appears in its small things: a corner newsstand, a shabby subway entrance, a street light illuminating a fragment of a familiar neighborhood, traffic signals flooding rain-washed pavement with luminous red and green, a manhole cover emitting lively wisps of steam, blinking neon signs, torn posters on a hoarding, the pattern of a sidewalk, the texture of a wall.

These small things add up to something as far-reaching as the city itself; they are the conveyers of the intimate and special character by which it is known. Familiar, omnipresent, oddly personal, they create the local color of the local scene. They are the humble, utilitarian objects without which no community can survive—the common conveniences and services that are the small-scale trade-marks of the urban world. Nor are we indifferent to their effect. What sentimental attachments have been formed for London's street lamps! What international affection exists for Parisian kiosks and Roman fountains! Not long ago, an English book firm in New York imported a London lamppost for a literary cocktail party that required an atmosphere of proper British nostalgia. And it is the British, too, who have coined the succinct, appropriate term for these ubiquitous outdoor accoutrements: "Street Furniture."

Street furniture, referred to also as "Things in Streets" and "Things Outdoors," has been somewhat drearily defined as the necessary objects used to equip the space around and

between buildings. It includes street lamps and street names, the poles, graceful or grotesque, that carry them, traffic lights, mailboxes, phone booths, litter baskets, ash receivers, fire hydrants, subway shelters, bus stops, benches, planting boxes, stanchions, signals, signs, fountains, memorials, statues, and small utilitarian structures—the complete inventory of items with which we grace, or disgrace, the outdoor scene. For beyond its usefulness, street furniture can be handsome, hideous, tidy, chaotic, suitable, unsuitable, cheerful, or depressing. Significantly, whether it is any or all of these things has little to do with its age or locale.

The dramatic modern street lights for the town of Vällingby, Sweden, and the lighting designs of the 1870's for the New York City Park Department (both illustrated above) are good to look at, each in its own way. Yet the gawky, massive standards recently erected as part of the "beautification" program of New York's Third Avenue are distressingly ugly, their obtrusive bad design out of all proportion to whatever improvements in illumination have been gained. New York's International Airport, on the other hand, has turned a forest of newly designed light standards that might have been a foot-candle catastrophe into an area of graceful glitter because the fixtures have been studied for looks as well as function, to make a pleasing pattern of orderly, repetitive shapes (also shown above).

The neatness of most European street signs, fastened

MUSEUM OF CITY OF N.Y.; MASS. DEPT. OF COMMERCE; MUSEUM OF CITY OF N.Y.; EWING GALLOWAY; MARVIN KONER; FROM *Sweden Builds*, G. E. KIDDER-SMITH; COURTESY I. M. PEI & ASSOCIATES; EMMA LANDAU

| STREET, CHICAGO, TODAY | VALLINGBY, SWEDEN, TODAY | ZECKENDORF PLAZA, DENVER, TODAY | N. Y. INTERNATIONAL AIRPORT |

simply to building walls, points up the chaotic confusion of the catchall American street pole, which overwhelms its name sign with a welter of mismatched, miscellaneous information. In historic districts, like Boston's Beacon Hill and the Vieux Carré of New Orleans, suitability has outscored technical advance in the selection of street furniture—lighting standards in particular—for the sake of a style compatible with the architecture. Other areas jar the pedestrian with overpowering, monster-from-Mars fixtures and gross overillumination in an obsessive and questionable attempt to reproduce daylight levels of brightness (see the example from Chicago, above). Street furniture in the best of America's huge new shopping centers is co-ordinated with a careful design sense for clarity, attractiveness, and occasional sheer delight. In contrast, the grand, arcaded shopping streets of the late nineteenth century—the dusty avenues of Turin, for example —are monstrously overscaled in accordance with the delusions of grandeur of Victorian city planning, and are badly lit from comic-opera lamps or cold new neon tubes to achieve an extraordinarily depressing effect.

Good, bad or indifferent, one fact about all street furniture is incontrovertibly clear: it is inescapable. It clutters outdoor space as surely as chairs and tables clutter houses and is subject to the same vagaries of taste and fashion, often with the same deplorable results. In spite of its omnipresence and its undeniable effect on people and places, however, we seldom

think of it as something that can be controlled, or as one of the arts of design. Like trees or Topsy, we believe that it just grew—and in a sense, it did. As urban existence became more elaborate and artificial, its necessary adjuncts became more numerous and involved. The wide-open spaces are no longer wide nor open, but crowded with signs and services; the sidewalks of New York, Paris, London, St. Louis, or Des Moines are a confusion of disorderly "conveniences."

In addition, the conquest of the city by the automobile has required special provisions for traffic regulation: an endless multiplication of directions, admonitions, and warnings superimposed on a fine frenzy of pre-existing street signs, police, fire, and sanitation department instructions, with no co-ordination of lettering, color, size, shape, or style. To this confusion we add the inevitable unplanned accumulation of routine outdoor facilities. Sometimes, in a burst of civic consciousness, we also add planting boxes; the effect is of roses in bedlam. A few years ago, in protest, New York's Museum of Modern Art made an object lesson of a representative service grouping at the corner of Fifth Avenue and 53rd Street, displaying a giant photograph of it, unretouched and unglamorized, in the purity of one of its orderly white galleries. For those who cared, its message was satisfactorily shocking. The street-corner clutter photographed four blocks south on Madison Avenue for the opening page of this article shows some newer additions, but says the same thing. Unfortunately, it is

107

Outdoor benches range from the utilitarian in New York today (above) to a fanciful design of the 1870's for the city's Central Park (upper right) and a new departure in Cuernavaca, Mexico (right), providing shade.

not until the mishandling of these outdoor elements becomes glaringly obvious that we notice, or object.

Assuming that we do notice, what do we learn? First, we become aware of the truth of no design, or of maldesign, of most of the elements of the urban environment. We are made conscious, perhaps for the initial time, of the fact that street furniture is planned and installed as a public service, deliberately designed for better or for worse, and that much of it could be considerably better. Those who have the advantage of visual training—artists, designers, architects— are aware of a good deal more. An Italian architect visiting New York made a remarkable and revealing photographic record of the "floor" of the city—the infinite patterns and styles of pavement, curbings, and manhole covers like "iron flowers" in the asphalt streets, that together compose striking effects of design and accident ordinarily lost beneath hurrying feet. There are other things, less subtle, that cannot possibly escape us. Certain aspects of the outdoor scene—the shopping street, for example, with its signs and store fronts competing boldly for attention—make constant, insistent demands upon our senses. The lesson here is unavoidable. Lack of design leads to total visual anarchy: the strident confusion of lettering, light, color, and scale typical of streets like New York's Sixth Avenue (page 111) or downtown Los Angeles' Hill Street. Co-ordinated design gives us all-too-rare

visual pleasure: Copenhagen's Tivoli Gardens, for instance (page 111), where antiquarian symbols of considerable charm and elegance are employed to do the job of shop signs, or, in more modern terms, the bright, attractive patterns of contemporary lettering and color in today's better shopping centers, like Victor Gruen's Eastland and Northland developments in Detroit or his Southdale near Minneapolis.* The quality of our environment, it soon becomes apparent, is directly related to our attention to it.

Second, we discover that we are not alone in our concern. For at least ten years preceding general American involvement in the matter, British professional magazines—*The Architectural Review* and *Design*—have attacked the problem of street furniture. *The Architectural Review* expanded the theme of "Things Outdoors" (from "Things in Streets" to "Things in Fields") as far as possible, with a dramatic, special-issue blast at the large-scale despoliation of the English countryside through man-made changes and additions, calling it, with gentlemanly upper-case fury, "OUTRAGE." Meanwhile *Stile Industria,* the Italian design magazine, has written critically of *"La Strada Come Ambiente"* (the street as environment). The Architectural League of New York has

*For illustrations of Victor Gruen's Southdale, see the article "Metropolis Regained" in HORIZON for July, 1959.

The romanticism of an early New York Central Park arbor (upper left) and the playfulness of Antonio Gaudí's parapet seats in Barcelona (left) contrast with the severity of a contemporary "exedra" in Cleveland (above).

tackled the subject through discussion and exhibition, stressing the architect's and designer's responsibilities. Professionals everywhere, intensely interested in the problem, have demonstrated a marked zeal for the promotion of good design for civic betterment.

"Good," however, is too often equated with "new," and "new" with that consistently misunderstood euphemism that covers a multitude of abuses—"progress." Since the old is automatically undesirable by this dubious reasoning, the result, even among conscientious professionals, is an overstressed tendency toward "out with the old and in with the new," regardless of consequences. If we are not to fall into this common error of thinking (or, more accurately, nonthinking), it is essential that we learn to differentiate not just between new and old, but to distinguish between the beautiful and the ordinary—independent of period or style. The inability to so distinguish, and to evaluate each on its own proper merits, stems partly from the fact that the modern movement has promoted newness on a basis of inexorable moral rightness. Its prophets, many of whom wear a marked sainted air, have adopted that familiar pair of traditional virtues, cleanliness and godliness. "Clean" design, we are told, is simple, uncluttered, straightforward, functional, and logical —and therefore good. Nor can we argue with this premise. In the name of good modern design many clean, functional,

logical solutions for lighting, seating, and sundry civic services have been developed. Alas, some of these designs are as ugly, or uglier than the older items that they replace! We are beginning to suspect, while paying tribute to acknowledged masterpieces in the contemporary style, that beauty is more than a matter of a rational approach. Stripped simplicity and carefully calculated line, in the hands of today's talented young men, can produce superb results, but the young men of earlier centuries, working with curlicue and ormolu, were no less acquainted with the secrets of aesthetic success.

Witness two equally competent "exedrae" (shaded outdoor seats); one of the nineteenth, the other of the twentieth century. Today's example, designed by the architects Mayer, Whittlesey & Glass for developer James H. Scheuer's Longwood Village in Cleveland, Ohio, is simple, suitable, and slightly antiseptic. The earlier example, for New York's Central Park, is less simple, just as suitable, and adds the unexpected delight of fantasy in its elaborately interlaced tree forms. (Both are shown on page 109.) No one with a proper understanding of the fact that design must be a product of its own times, attitudes, and technology would advocate emulating the solutions of the past. This way lie boredom, sterility, and a cultural dead end. And yet, the clean, contemporary counterpart of the Victorian extravaganza is strangely disappointing. Strictly businesslike, its one foray

MUSEUM OF MODERN ART; GARTH HUXTABLE; SABINE WEISS—
RAPHO-GUILLUMETTE; COURTESY I. M. PEI & ASSOCIATES

Individuality in street furniture: left, entrances to the Paris Metro (turn of century) and New York's subway (c. 1913); above, a Paris advertising kiosk and its echo in a shopping center on Long Island.

into fancy is relegated to a pregnant pole just beyond the shelter by designer Leo Lionni, which houses, with rather grim levity, a clock and a loudspeaker. (The privilege of public silence is another of today's lost joys.)

If art is more than good intentions, good street furniture is obviously more than the mere fulfillment of its necessary functions. It is, as already implied, a source of civic improvement and public pleasure and pride. To achieve these ends requires a thorough understanding of the special characteristics of public design. We might begin by listing a few things that useful street furniture, correctly conceived, is not. It is not a dominating ornament for its surroundings. This role is reserved for sculpture, fountains, and memorials, where other values than primary utility are stressed. It should not be the self-conscious declaration of the personality of the designer, advertising his ingenuity and originality to the world. Nothing is in poorer taste than the strident insistence on the designer as an individual, for a captive audience in a public place. One might say that the best street furniture is most remarkable for its unobtrusiveness. Nor is this the negative statement that it seems. For unobtrusiveness does not mean dullness. It is a subtle blend of suitability to purpose, harmony with locale, and low-key, but definite, visual pleasure. To accomplish all this, and still be clearly visible

and identifiable, is a neat trick of taste and talent, far more difficult than recourse to eye-catching gimmicks.

These requirements were often better understood by older generations, when undeniable decorative flamboyance was wedded to a romantic respect for nature, and by extension, for the setting. Today, we consider the design tour de force more important than its relationship to the people who must use it, or the site that must receive it. We forget that street furniture is the most personal and human element of the urban scene—and potentially the most irritating. Its unavoidable intimacy suggests soft-voiced, sympathetic design, rather than false monumentality or overstated "styling." Yet contemporary designers of considerable reputation do not hesitate to offer forced excursions into startling pseudo-modernism for public services, good for little but announcing the aesthetic up-to-dateness of the creator. Highly touted solutions, like Chicago's new State Street lighting standards (pages 106–107), confuse and vulgarize the direct modern approach to create a style that might be called "contemporary corn." Outdoor signs, overanxious to break with tradition, proffer information with insistent lower-case archness when simple, Roman-lettered dignity might be preferable. Outdoor play equipment, borrowing the shapes of abstract sculpture for free-form crawl-throughs or climb-arounds, is often

Design, LONDON; EWING KRAININ; EMMA LANDAU

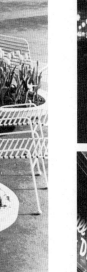

Grace, charm, and clutter: above, London planting boxes set up for the 1951 Festival of Britain; upper right, old shop signs in Copenhagen's Tivoli Gardens; right, Sixth Avenue chaos, New York.

ludicrously grotesque for its purpose and place. All of these so-called modern designs are no more than mannerisms derived from legitimate modern art, and they are aggressively antagonistic to their surroundings.

We will have taken a giant step toward the improvement of our streets and cities when we cease our unquestioning endorsement of all that is new at the expense of all that is old. For variety is not only the spice of life but of the outdoor environment as well. The basic standards—suitability, harmony, and pleasure—apply equally to the products of the present and the past, and there is no reason why we should not have the best of both worlds. The spread between the street furniture provided by different generations is often a desirable and interesting one. It tells much of people, tastes, and times, and enriches the cultural and visual aspects of a city. Standardization, always advisable from the viewpoint of efficiency and economy, is the enemy of the infinite, legendary pleasures of the unique. New York's current plan to replace its many models of lighting fixtures, of almost as many different dates, with a new, uniform design will undoubtedly provide better light in more places, but it will also leave the city aesthetically and historically much poorer.

The handsome entrances, symbols, and signs of the London Underground are a superior example of contemporary street furniture design. The much older *art nouveau* entrances and kiosks of the Paris Metro, Hector Guimard's strange, sinuous, plantlike structures of the beginning of the century, are equally attractive (page 110). So much so, in fact, that The Museum of Modern Art in New York has acquired a Metro gate as part of its permanent design collection. Antonio Gaudí's fantastic serpentine seats in Barcelona's Park Güell (page 109), built from 1900 to 1914, add character and luster to that city today. To the art-conscious tourist (and art in one form or another is largely what tourism is all about) Guimard's Metro and Gaudí's park rank as special attractions. Even New York's grimy and dishonored subway kiosks (page 110) can be seen as structures of considerable design interest. The numerous ornate exercises in cast iron with which our cities still abound—notably lamp standards and public seating—have particular significance as a survival of our grandfathers' preoccupation with a blossoming industrial technology, and the once proud material that left its mark on every design effort from the dome of the United States Capitol to park benches around the world. These metallic ribbons, rosettes, and rococo convolutions were as "modern" in their day as the severely elegant lights and sleek slab benches of Denver's recently constructed Zeckendorf Plaza by architect I. M. Pei (page 107). Both are true

111

GERALD CINAMON; SHIRLEY GLASER; EMMA LANDAU

expressions of the taste and technology of their times. To eliminate these natural contrasts of structure and style is to lose a large part of the authentic drama of the city scene.

Undeniably, a great deal becomes obsolescent with the passage of years. If changes are inevitable, however, it is not too much to ask that discretion and judgment be exercised in making them. It might be advisable to consider first whether destruction of the old is always an unavoidable necessity. If contemporary needs and technological advances make replacement mandatory, then new, clearly contemporary designs can be evolved, keeping in mind the desirable criteria already mentioned. For we are faced with no small problem in our twentieth-century cities; growth and revolutionary civic patterns are working a radical transformation of entire communities, and all of the services and facilities involved. City planning, a modern science, has been charged with the redevelopment of centers destroyed or damaged in the war, and of entire new towns. Cities-in-creation, like Brasilia, the still incomplete capital of Brazil, and Chandigarh, the new capital of the East Punjab in India, are phenomena of our time; they will provide, beyond buildings and roads, all of the urban utilities as well.

Fortunately, we are not without preparation for the task. Today's conditions have supplied unique experimental laboratories for the design of street furniture: the housing development, the shopping center, and the international fair. In these isolated, rather artificial instances, it has been possible to create a small new world. Expositions like the Festival of Britain, in 1951, the 1958 Brussels Exposition, and this summer's Moscow Fair, new town-size shopping units, and housing schemes of community scope have provided unusual opportunities for undertaking the development and co-ordination of outdoor facilities on an unprecedented scale. Beyond the job of the designer, however, the responsibility for the appearance of the necessary equipment of our cities and towns is, to a surprising extent, our own.

If we are to stem the tide of "Horrors Outdoors," we would do well to learn to look at our streets and to see clearly what we have put there. The observing eye becomes a critical eye, and public taste sets public standards. Only by developing perceptive, critical awareness can we hope for greater order and aesthetic quality in this important area of public design.

Ada Louise Huxtable, contributing editor of Progressive Architecture, Arts, *and* Art in America, *has been working on a Guggenheim Fellowship for a study of structural and design advances in American building.*

Love According to Madison Avenue

Today's copy writer creates his own canon of passion as he links almost every product to springs of romance

In studying the love life of the ancient Romans, I have been struck by the fact that some of the sharpest and most illuminating evidence comes not from weighty works of history but from wayward and trivial sources. A lustful *graffito* scratched on a marble column, palpitating for the scarred arms of a gladiator; indecorous decorations on the bedroom walls of a seaside villa; a versified book of cosmetic recipes; a sentimental funeral oration carved on a huge tombstone—these are the real voices of the past.

It occurs to me, therefore, that in our own time the sociologists with their ponderous surveys, the psychologists with their dissecting analyses, and the cultural historians with their masses of documentation may be missing the truth and the essence of modern love. Perhaps those who write the contemporary equivalent of *graffiti* come closer. I suggest that the persons who do so are those who scribble on Madison Avenue—not on the building fronts, to be sure, but on typewriter paper, in air-conditioned cubicles in the well-carpeted offices of B.B.D. & O., K. & E., Y. & R., E.W.R. & R., and so on.

Certainly they see a number of truths about American love that have never been reported in the scientific literature. For one thing, the ad men apparently perceive more clearly than anyone else just how deeply love has penetrated and colored the ordinary routine of American life, until a number of formerly nonerotic objects have become associated with the most tender scenes and the most romantic moments. Eating utensils, for example, are not thought by most cultural historians to have any love-value, and even the Freudians see symbolism only in the knife. But the ad men for Oneida silverware are more acute reporters of the local scene. In a recent ad in *Mademoiselle* they recorded the spontaneous love-dialogue of two young people examining a teaspoon at a store counter:

She: It's a dream come true, Bob. . . . I thought we'd <u>never</u> find it. Now we could almost choose blindfolded—just by following our hearts.

He: Looks as if <u>both</u> our hearts are set on "Lasting Spring"—it's a "forever thing," like our marriage!

Paolo and Francesca were moved by a poem, Tristan and Iseult by a potion, but with young lovers in America it is the sight of a four-piece place setting at $18 (plus Federal tax) that unlocks the gates of the heart.

Similarly, it is the writers of fashion copy who see through the shadows and mists of native puritanism and recognize that the shoe, which traditionally has played no recognized part in American love-making, has recently acquired an aura of erotic value such as it has not had since Solomon, or whoever wrote the *Song of Solomon*, sang the finest bit of advertising copy yet: "How beautiful are thy feet with shoes, O prince's daughter!" In a comparably rapturous vein, the Wohl Shoe Company of St. Louis offered young women, via the February 15, 1959, issue of *Vogue*, a pump described as a "dream of a shoe," and spelled out the dream visually: a lovely young miss leaned upon the manly chest of a masked

By MORTON M. HUNT

caballero. No prosaic considerations of arch support or hygienic insole for her; the shoe is no longer a piece of utilitarian clothing, but a *laissez-passer* to the wondrous fantasy world of romance. Underwear, too, according to the testimony of the Madison Avenue confraternity, has an equally transporting effect. A case in point is a message some of them produced for Seamprufe, Inc. in a recent issue of *Seventeen*. In this instance, the journey took place in time as well as in space: the ad showed a medieval knight in chain mail, mounted upon a white charger, in the act of sweeping up with one arm a damsel improbably clad only in a lace-trimmed slip of nylon tricot. If, indeed, lingerie produces such reveries in American women, one can only be struck with admiration at the strength of character they show in getting past the state of deshabille and actually arriving at their jobs or starting their housework.

Like shoes and slips, it would seem that many liquids which formerly were thirst quenchers have also picked up amorous overtones in recent years. Coca-Cola was for decades a drink that made merely for a refreshing pause; nowadays, we learn, it is also an accoutrement of teen-age love-trysts. In the April issue of *Seventeen,* for example, a Coke ad shows lad and lass, carrying a bagful of Coke, looking for a picnic spot; finding it, they shed some outer clothes and open a couple of Cokes; this causes them at once to fall tenderly upon each other's bosom, ecstatically guzzling, preparatory to nuzzling.

Even more noteworthy is the instance of beer. This drink was once the hearty, indelicate, eructative refreshment of the hard-working plebeian male. It has apparently undergone a marvelous metamorphosis in recent years, becoming not only suitable for delicate lips, but acquiring an aura of enchantment and romance. A series of Schlitz advertisements in several major magazines has shown young couples parked by a lakeside at twilight, alone on a snow-capped mountaintop, and so on. Young, attractive, and clearly drawn to each other, they are always drinking beer out of one glass; these lovers, and their circumstances, exemplify the hedonistic exhortation under the picture: "Know the real joy of good living." This, to be sure, could refer either to the romance or the beer; the ad is not explicit. Nor can one be sure whether romance inspired a desire for beer or beer a desire for romance. One thing *is* indisputable: the distinctive odor of hops, now found upon the attractive female, must have been reclassified in the national aesthetic system, becoming a scent rather than a smell.

Other procedures, once gustatory, have likewise become amatory, or so it would seem. The smoking of tobacco, long thought appropriate to manly work or solitary reflection, has become almost obligatory at times of flirtation or intimacy. From the ubiquitous scenes of nubile young people igniting their little white tubes, one gains the impression that drawing in a lungful of soot and carcinogens has an amorous value as great as once did the reading aloud of Byron or the strumming of a banjo. Amatory smoking does present one awkward problem, however, since countless ads (not by cigarette makers) report that love is inconceivable unless the mouth and breath are totally unsullied. Once again the problem is solved by a reshuffling of the national stimulus-response bonds, until smoke, on the breath, becomes exciting; the old proverb should really be altered to read: "Where there is smoke, there will soon be fire." Let no one find fault with this or make mock of it. Do not lovers in the Trobriand Islands extract and eat lice from one other's hair, becoming mightily inflamed with love by the procedure? If, in the liberal spirit of cultural relativism, one accepts this and refuses to find it revolting, should he not do the same in the case of the reeking Americans?

Still, Americans themselves have not yet altogether succeeded in eroticizing the by-products of smoking, as Madison Avenue itself admits. A remarkably candid ad for Parliament cigarettes recently came right out about the risk to amorous aesthetics: man and girl were shown, heads thrillingly close together, match lit for their cigarettes, while the copy, drawing attention to the recessed filter, promised in a throaty aside, "No filter feedback on your lips . . . or hers." Love in America in 1959 is evidently not for the oaf, but for the thoughtful practitioner of methodology. Ovid himself, that dedicated professor of tasteful dalliance, would have recognized in the Parliament copy writer a kindred spirit, a fellow toiler in the vineyards of impeccable passion.

Again and again the ad men indicate how easily Americans are aroused to lust or moved to tenderness by formerly non-erotic consumer products. Consider the vitamins offered in *Cosmopolitan* by the Vitasafe Corporation: their effect is plainly amorous, for the middle-aged couple are snuggling happily while the woman confesses, from an overflowing heart, "He made me feel like a bride again." Consider the electric portable offered by Smith-Corona: a book-laden youth passing a pretty girl looks down at her typewriter with a mooncalf expression, but it is clear that the machine has made him tender towards the girl as well. Consider fudge, of all things: Carnation Evaporated Milk shows a lass plastering it on cupcakes, while a crewcut lad eats one out of her hand, the plain implication being that fudge is an important component of her sex appeal.

This point is not spelled out in so many words, but sometimes obscurity is in itself a species of truth. The Marlboro people have been portraying rugged middle-aged sporting types lighting cigarettes for lovely young things; in small type under each such picture is the cryptic text, "The cigarette designed for men that women like." The Delphic Oracle herself might have written it; parse it and puzzle over it as one will, he cannot be sure whether the "that" liked by the young thing is the cigarette designed for men, or the men themselves. But the truth lies not in deciding which one; the answer is that it means *both* of them, for they are blended in her mind and emotions. *That* is the truth the copy writer was conveying —in the prevailing romantic American landscape, the erotic object and the erotic person have become indistinguishable.

Precisely the same conclusion may be drawn from Pan American World Airways' appeal to businesswomen in *Mademoiselle*. "Look what Jet Clippers can do for your dreams," it reads, and illustrates what it means: the young businesswoman is seated on a hillside with a morsel of Roman ruin behind her and a dark-haired handsome man beside her. What is the dream referred to—the man or the *mise-en-scène?* Possibly the text gives a further clue. "The fun of new experiences comes faster on Pan Am wings," it says. No help there; that still fits either one. But does it really matter? Not in the least: the trip abroad, the Roman ruin, the handsome man are all inseparable and indivisible. Love and the product are two aspects of a single essence; that is all they know on Madison Avenue, and all they need to know.

Within this general picture of American love, as set down by the creative men in the copy and art departments of the major agencies, no detail is more intriguing than the observation that contemporary Americans, though supposedly scornful of occultism, rely upon a variety of philters, amulets, talismans, potions, and brews, without which love is unattainable.

It is, of course, no secret to anyone that the normal exudates of the human body, the wrinkles that come after youth, and such other common characteristics as dull hair, small breasts, plumpness, and blackheads are totally incompatible with affection and sex, and that no person with any of these defects can possibly find happiness in life. Luckily there is available today a splendid armamentarium of lotions, oils, paddings, pills, cleansers, and paints the use of which obviates the fault and admits the user to the arena of love.

But this is only the surface of truth. A closer inspection of advertising art and copy reveals a far subtler message being set down for all to read who are not willfully blind. If I read it rightly, there would appear to be, in modern love, a mysterious disembodiment of emotion: it is not so much the *beauti-*

ful person who is loved, but the *beautifying instrumentality*. Observe the statement made repeatedly in ads for Coty's "L'Aimant": "Nothing makes a woman more feminine to a man. . . ." What exegesis can there be, except that the femininity is in the bottled liquid, and not, basically, in the woman? And the same brand of metaphysics must lie behind the Lanvin ad which shows a small boy kissing a small girl who, though pleased, admits to herself: "He loves me . . . he loves my Mommy's Arpege!" The artful minx knows the truth; only by virtue of the applied balsam is she a nymphet, and he, willy-nilly, a nympholept.

The female of all ages is continually advised that she need only wipe on this unguent, pat on this fragrance, slip on this magical garment, and lo! he sees with new eyes, thinks with a different brain, loses his own purpose and becomes a willing slave. "If he can't make up his mind . . . wear Wind Song," whispers Prince Matchabelli. Lanvin slyly peddles the same kind of bottled powers, offering them with the tag, "How to make him lose the first round!" And let a woman but slip into a marvelous checked suit made by Junior Sophisticates, and, she is advised, "What can he do but surrender. . . ."

All this has a disturbingly supernatural sound, yet a hauntingly familiar one. What *is* it all an echo of? What old, well-known, half-forgotten nightmare? So musing, one may recall that there *were* women once who cloaked themselves in borrowed beauty to steal the love of man—sinful women who compacted with Satan to receive unlawful powers, and in return did his vile work for him. Suddenly, certain words and phrases in advertising copy, seemingly harmless, begin to assume an ominous sound. Danskin, Inc., who make a lounging outfit modeled after ballet costumes, use the telltale phrase, "for your 'at home' *bewitching* hours" (my italics). For being bewitching, 30,000 women were burned alive during the fifteenth and sixteenth centuries; * let the word not go by unnoticed. And Dawnelle, Inc. frankly (or is it carelessly?) harks back to woman's ancient primal alliance with the Prince of Darkness in both copy and illustration. Says the copy: "You're the temptress who wins him, in Dawnelle's handsewn gloves"; the illustration, meanwhile, shows not one, but four gloved female hands offering a fatuously grinning male four ripe apples. (Has Eve grown more arms, or is the Serpent in an arms race too?)

And now the most damning fact begins to appear more clearly. In distinct defiance of the overtly approved mores, the entrapment or illusion created almost always operates within a context of illicit connection. The ads for a hundred products hint at it, but those of the perfume makers are

*See "The Persecution of Witches" on page 57 of this issue.

115

practically outspoken. The names of perfumes are in themselves an insidious and deadly attack upon Judeo-Christian morality—e.g., "Tabu," "Indiscrete," "Conquête," "Temptation," "Surrender," and "My Sin"—while the copy strengthens the assault in words such as these:

"danger in every drop"

"the 'forbidden' fragrance"

"provocative as a stranger's smile"

"dare to wear it only when you seek to conquer"

"a whispered invitation for a man to be masterful."

One could extract from all this a sinister truth, namely that woman descended of Eve is still borrowing powers and enchantments in order to arouse man's lusts and thereby satisfy her own, and in the process is performing Satan's work of dragging man into mortal sin. Six centuries ago the best-educated men in Europe considered the situation a clear and present danger and spoke of it in terms like these:

In the woman wantonly adorned to capture souls, the garland upon her head is as a firebrand of Hell to kindle men, so too the horned headdress of another, so the brooch upon the breast [of a third]. . . . Each is a spark, breathing hellfire [and] damning the souls God has created and redeemed at such great cost.

Thus spoke John Bromyard, a typical fourteenth-century English preacher and compiler of sermons, and thus had spoken in earlier times Tertullian, Jerome, and Chrysostom. Today none but advertising men link the same factors in a single picture of woman; but whether the ad men are the Bromyards and Tertullians of our era or whether they are agents of the Foul Fiend is not altogether clear.

The seductive female is not the only pattern of womanhood about which Madison Avenue furnishes an abundance of information. The other and sharply contrasting pattern is that of the fiancée-wife-mother. The ancient dichotomy of Woman into Eve and Mary, mistress and mother, witch and lady, apparently did not disappear with the end of feudalism but lives on still, according to the evidence at hand.

For whenever the female in an advertisement is alluring and beguiling, whenever her smile is secretive and mysterious, she represents the ancient spirit of Profane Love and her mystery is, ultimately, nothing but concupiscence. But when woman is portrayed in the role of fiancée, bride, or wife, she possesses none of these qualities; instead she is feminine in a pure and wholesome sense. The American Gem Society, addressing an ad to the girl about to become engaged, portrays her as a dreaming young thing, chin cupped in hands, wide eyes staring off into the roseate future, guileless face almost completely innocent of make-up, mouth smiling trustfully and a little wistfully. She is Everyman's kid sister or girl friend, but never his passionflower. The Kinsey crowd may publish their revolting statistics on the premarital sexual experiences of American girls, but the advertisements tell a different and lovelier version of the truth: the girl who gets a diamond engagement ring has not been besmirched by sexual experiments, or known the indecent hunger of desire.

Even in the embrace of her fiancé she preserves a high-minded concentration upon nonsexual matters. A dinnerware ad in *Seventeen* shows a young couple who have ridden in a sleigh out to a secluded field through which runs a purling stream. The lad romantically picks up the girl in his arms and carries her across the virgin snow, while she tenderly and practically murmurs to him, "You get the license . . . I'll get the Lenox." His intentions may have been licentious rather than licensable, but this comment at once purifies and clarifies his mind.

Nuptials and honeymoon make no perceptible change in this side of her character; the bride's mood may be yielding, but her blood runs cool. "Isn't this how you want to live?" asks the Fostoria Glass Company, portraying an ideal young marriage: a young wife, holding a piece of crystal stemware near a single burning taper, seems lost in admiration of the glass and the candle, and only vaguely aware of the handsome husband hovering beside her. She is smiling at him, more or less, with her neat, childish little mouth firmly closed—and a generation trained by Marilyn Monroe does not miss the significance of *that*. Not long ago a Heublein Cocktails ad in *Life* featured what seems merely an amusing line—"A wife's warmest welcome is well chilled"; like so many other jokes, perhaps it says more than it intends to.

After a suitable time, the wife becomes a mother, but despite this presumptive evidence of sexual activity, she remains thoroughly pure. In a Vigoro ad we see her romping on the lawn with her husband and children; she is tanned, healthy, and essentially *friendly*. In a Johnson outboard motor ad we see her roaring along with her husband and children in a speedboat; she is sunburned, tousled, and essentially a *good sport*. In a G-E ad we see her clapping her hands gleefully as her husband and daughter present her with a dishwasher; she is slim, pretty (in a low-heeled way), and essentially *homey*.

We see her in many other situations—cooking, washing, shopping, playing games—and she is almost invariably clean-looking, hearty, efficient, and brightly lit. Dan River Mills recently devoted a spread in *Life* to the modern American family and showed four typical examples. Every one of the four consisted of a handsome young man, a pretty young woman, and two children (between the ages of four and eight), all dressed in cottons by Dan River. In not one picture is the man touching, holding, or even looking at his wife; in three out of four, he is not even standing beside her, but is separated from her by one of the children. The American wife, it seems reasonable to conclude, is a pal, a helpmeet, a kind of older girl friend; she is emphatically not a lover.

The children have a double function in preserving the mother-image: they prove her fecundity, but by their very presence they neutralize or purify the erotic overtones of certain situations. Do she and her husband don Weldon pajamas?—in come the kids, in similar pajamas, making everything sanitary and aboveboard. Does she go off for a ride with her man in a Chrysler prod- uct?—she tucks a little girl into her lap, and all is sweet, all is sound. Do she and he park their Chevrolet in a secluded woodland spot?—hap- pily, they brought the dog along, and it is upon the beast that affec- tion is bestowed. Have she and her husband grown cheerfully middle- aged and regained their privacy as the children left home?—the Gen- eral Motors time-payment plan shows them hugging *two* dogs, one for each. No wonder the dog is called man's best friend—he defends, by his very presence, the purity of the American wife and mother.

Certain other aspects of American love, though not so fully portrayed, are illuminatingly touched upon in magazine advertisements. For it is apparent from any care- ful scrutiny of the ads that Americans require the stimulus of exotic, remote, or uncomfortable surroundings, in order to experience the real transports of delight. Here is an advertisement showing a couple on a wild, chilly-looking beach at sundown (how *did* they get that auto- mobile down there without making tracks in the sand?); here is another couple deep in the forest primeval, smoking cigarettes and hugging each other; here is a third exploring a wild stream bank in their good clothing, undaunted by steep declivity or tangled underbrush. Oasis Cigarettes render continual reports of lovers cozily nestled on a desert cactus, moodily bussing each other in some dim alley of the Vieux Carré of New Orleans, or perching together in a high win- dow overlooking Monte Carlo. They never wax romantic in Middletown, U.S.A.; they never grow fond in a middle-class living room. Wind-swept Alpine crags, the slippery decks of heeled-over yawls, castles without plumbing, streams in the heart of a jungle—these would seem to be the typical loci

DRAWINGS BY CHARMATZ

of love, rather than the sofa, bed, or park bench. How all this may be possible—since most people are forced to spend their lives at or near home—is a nagging question; perhaps the meaning of it all is that love, in the twentieth century, is an actuality for the wealthy, but still only a dream for the poor and the middle class.

Likewise tantalizing are the occasional hints of restiveness and impending revolt on the part of modern man. Ensnared and bewitched by the minx, captured and domesticated by the wife, does he begin nowadays to stir in his chains, re- membering the olden days? Drummond Knitwear, in *The New York Times*, portrays two sturdy upright chaps clad in knitted shirts, with a luscious female supine at their feet. Can it be mere coincidence that the Cigar Institute of Amer- ica shows a manly stogy-fancier hefting a caveman's club, while a maiden clad in a leopardskin crouches adoringly at heel? No, it is not coincidence, for here again is Chief Apparel, in *Playboy*, showing us a Bikini-clad morsel sprawled pantingly on the floor before a gen- tleman clad in dashing sports attire. But perhaps the significant clue is that in all three advertisements the gentlemen are ignoring the females. Woman is a toy (the ad men seem to be saying)—a plaything to be en- joyed when man chooses, and to be scorned when he does not.

Finally, and most challenging of all, is the handful of frivolous and irreverent remarks in recent adver- tisements that may conceivably por- tend a general devaluation of love in the near future. Hanes Hosiery in *The New Yorker* shows us a cartoon of a depressed chap clutching a bottle of poison and thinking, "I'd better drink it. All she wants from me is seamless stockings by Hanes." One does not get flippant about God or the Flag; perhaps Love, long the peer of both of these, is losing its position. A Lea & Perrins ad shows a man and woman curled up warmly together, just after dinner; it is the best of all possible times for serious talk, but listen to what she says: "Do you love Lea & Perrins more than me?" Is nothing sacred to woman any longer, that she dares to jest at a time like this?

Whatever may be the ultimate meaning of all these things, one must congratulate the cultural historians of the future; a treasure of evidence is awaiting them, if they will but look away from the scientific studies and scholarly theses and pay attention to the scribblings on Madison Avenue.

Morton M. Hunt, author of the recently published Natural History of Love, *contributed the article "The Greatest of Courtly Lovers" to the September, 1950,* HORIZON.

The Bible as Divining Rod

TEXT CONTINUED FROM PAGE 10

Yadin's most famous exploits in Israel's war with the Arab states were achieved by his knowledge of the terrain of Palestine and by his having carefully studied the military campaigns which were carried out there in ancient times as described in the Bible. He has now applied his study of the Bible, and his reliance upon it, to archaeological campaigns.

Knowing that Solomon's architects and engineers followed a more or less uniform pattern in the fortifications they erected, Yadin reasoned that the gateway of Hazor should conform to the plan of the gateway of Megiddo, which had already been excavated by the Oriental Institute of the University of Chicago. When his excavations, using a very large technical staff and some two hundred workmen, got to the buried gate, Yadin traced on the surface of the ground what he felt had to be the general plan of the gateway. Some of his workmen may be forgiven for thinking that he was something of a magician when the actual excavations revealed that the gateway of Hazor conformed to the sketch he had made.

The boundaries of entire lands and the nature of their ancient civilizations can be made clear by following clues in the Bible. It is almost as if one waves a magic wand over a blank area of the earth, and it becomes filled with roads, cities, people, and all the paraphernalia of throbbing life.

It was formerly thought that the entire Southland or Negev of Palestine, comprising about half of its total territory, had always been an uninhabited wasteland. This assumption stemmed partly from bearing in mind only one of two major descriptions in the Bible of the extent of the kingdom of Israel. The one that everybody remembered reads: "And Judah and Israel dwelt safely, every man under his vine and fig tree, *from Dan even unto Beersheba*, all the days of Solomon" (I Kings 4:25). The description that no one paid much attention to, and that almost everyone was inclined to dismiss as an exaggeration, states that Solomon's territory extended *"from the entrance to Hamath to the Brook of Egypt"* (I Kings 8:65), which means from southern Syria to the major north-south, dry-stream-bed system of the Wadi el 'Arish dividing Sinai into two natural geographical parts.

Which of the statements dealing with Solomon's kingdom was true? It would seem from superficial examination of these two passages that our belief in the validity of historical memory in the Bible is untenable. The fact is, however, that both of these statements are literally correct. The "Dan to Beersheba" description refers to the comparatively lush, fertile interior of Solomon's kingdom. The "Brook of Egypt" passage includes the outer reaches which, archaeological investigation has demonstrated, Solomon controlled with an iron hand, as did some of his successors on the throne of Israel.

Even without archaeological corroboration, it could have been figured out from the Biblical evidence alone that Sol-

omon had to control the area between Beersheba and the Brook of Egypt, which comprises all of the Negev and half of Sinai, because otherwise he would not have been able to conduct and protect his far-flung enterprises. We know from I Kings 10:20–29 that Solomon was a horse trader of magnitude. He engaged in a three-cornered trade which involved shipping horses from the Asia Minor gateway of Hittite Cilicia to Egypt in return for chariots and other goods which he then disposed of in the markets of Syria for cash or crops he needed for Israel. His caravans had therefore to cross the wide and little-inhabited reaches of Sinai and the Negev. To protect them, he built rows of fortresses and police posts. To house them, he erected caravanseries. To provide water for them, he had cisterns dug. And the same arrangements had to be established to secure his line of communications with his distant outpost of Ezion-geber on the north shore of the Gulf of Aqaba, and to protect caravans such as that of the Queen of Sheba, which carried "spices and very much gold and precious stones" (I Kings 10:2) from Arabia to Jerusalem.

The things that Solomon had to do to maintain peace in the Negev and in the half of Sinai which belonged to Israel are mentioned specifically in the Bible as having been redone by one of his successors, Uzziah. When, many years and half a dozen kings after the establishment of the Judaean kingdom, he mounted the throne in Jerusalem, Uzziah set out to restore the power of Judah. He rebuilt Ezion-geber, which the Edomites had destroyed in the interval, and he gave it a new name, Eloth. We are told that Uzziah's name "spread even to the entrance of Egypt" (II Chronicles 26:6–8), which means that he regained complete control not only of all of the Negev but at least of that part of Sinai which is bounded by the Brook of Egypt and perhaps even of all of Sinai. To do all this, and to make travel and settlement possible in the Negev, Uzziah "built towers in the Wilderness [the Negev] and hewed out many cisterns . . ." (II Chronicles 26:10).

Long before we began our archaeological exploration of the Negev, we were certain from the pertinent Biblical passages that we would find fortresses and villages and cisterns, and traces of agriculture, and artifacts of ancient civilizations. There seemed to be clues in the Bible also of permanent occupation of the land there in the Age of Abraham.

The Bible did not mislead us. We found hundreds of cisterns, dug first in Judaean times to catch and hold the precious rainfall, which averages between eight and four inches a year in the northern and central parts of the Negev. Last spring, flying over the Negev, I saw them again, filled with the runoff from the spring rains—still watertight after twenty-five hundred years. From the air we could see also the remains of fortresses that Uzziah is credited with having built on the hilltops and could follow with our eyes the lines of the modern trails, identical with ancient tracks, leading from Beersheba to Ezion-geber in one direction and to Sinai and Egypt in the other. The information gleaned from the historical statements in the Bible had once again been confirmed.

The Bible beckons excitingly to many new sites for archaeological exploration in the Holy Land and all of the ancient Near East. We would like to know more of the Philistines, who loom so large in the Bible and who disappeared so completely from history. The Philistines were one of the sea peoples who reared the high civilization of Crete (Caphtor in Amos 9:7) and the neighboring islands. In the times of turmoil that destroyed the balance of powers in the Near East during the thirteenth and twelfth centuries B.C., they erupted into Asia Minor, overthrew the Hittite empire, challenged Egypt, and finally established themselves in Canaan, whose fertile land they long contested with the Israelites. The struggle was close and the nearness of Philistine victory, which would so greatly have changed world history, is recorded in the name they bequeathed to the land they failed to conquer—Palestine. Fragments of pottery have provided the only material clues to the Philistines' Greek origin, but their cities lie buried on the Canaan coast, promising rich rewards to archaeologists.

Who will find the gold mines of Ophir? We know from the Bible that Solomon's ships trading out of Ezion-geber sailed down the eastern arm of the Red Sea. "And they came to Ophir, and fetched from thence gold, four hundred and twenty talents and brought it to King Solomon" (I Kings 9:28). But Ophir remains a mystery. It could have been in southwestern Arabia or on the northeastern shore of Africa, or possibly in India. There is no doubt that it exists—but where?

Karl S. Twitchell has told us about an ancient gold mine in southwestern Arabia, called "Mahad Dhahab" ("the Cradle of Gold"), which may have been worked as early as Solomon's times. Its ancient dump heaps yielded profitable sums of gold when treated in modern times by the American Smelting and Refining Company. The examination by a competent archaeologist of pottery remains, which must exist there, might show that these mines were contemporary with Solomon's copper mines in the Wadi Araba.

There is no question but that the most amazing finds will be made in Arabia. A preview of the startling discoveries which certainly will occur there if political conditions permit has been provided by the fascinating sculptures in stone and copper uncovered several years ago in southwestern Arabia by Arabian expeditions of the American Foundation for the Study of Man. The excavators, Wendell Phillips and William F. Albright and their companions, had to flee for their lives to escape the fanaticism of the ruler of Yemen, but not before they had opened the doors to a great treasure house of the past. The limited number of sculptures and inscriptions they discovered have already thrown much light upon the high state of civilization in the kingdom of Sheba and related states before, during, and after the famous Queen of Sheba.

But it is not necessary to go very far afield to find treasures of high importance for our increased understanding of the

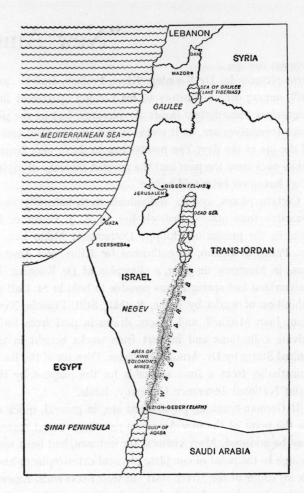

backgrounds of the Bible. Despite all the archaeological work done in the Holy Land proper, there is still vastly more to be undertaken there than has yet been accomplished. Phoenician temples and inscriptions in Palestine await discovery, as well as remains of the Hittites, whose origins and culture and language still remain largely a mystery to us. Abraham had already had dealings with them in the second millennium B.C. when he purchased the Cave of Machpelah in Hebron from them for a burial place (Genesis 23:3–20). And the whole land of Galilee still remains almost a virgin field for archaeological undertakings, although the Hebrew University excavations of Hazor are presently doing much to add to our knowledge of that region.

There are generations and centuries of additional work to be done in the field of Biblical archaeology in the Holy Land proper and in related lands. Many of the pointers to be followed and the places to be excavated are already mentioned in Sacred Scripture. They need only to be believed in and followed up, and there is no question but that the historical reward of pursuing them will be great.

Nelson Glueck is the president of the Hebrew Union College–Jewish Institute of Religion and for many years has directed archaeological expeditions in the Near East. In his book Rivers in the Desert *(Farrar, Straus, and Cudahy, 1959) he identifies Biblical sites uncovered in the Negev desert of Israel. The Biblical translations in the article are the author's own.*

"New American Painting"

CONTINUED FROM PAGE 41

owns pictures by De Kooning, Kline, Pollock, Rothko, and Still, among others. Visitors to his London apartment find themselves immediately *inside* the pictures, just as the pictures themselves are, as it seems to him, in the dead center of the life of the day. The painter has, in short, very largely taken over from the poet and the novelist the duty of saying what has never been said before.

Certain places, certain individuals were naturally more receptive than others. Brussels has an E. J. Power of its own, in the person of Philippe Dotremont; Milan has, in Dr. Panza di Biumo, an enthusiast for Kline, and Amsterdam, in Mevrouw de Jong, a champion of De Kooning. In Switzerland last spring it was possible to hold in St. Gall an exhibition of works by Kline, Rothko, Still, Francis, Newman, Joan Mitchell, and others, drawn in part from Swiss private collections and in part from works bought in the United States by Dr. Arnold Rüdlinger, Director of the Basle Kunsthalle, from a fund set aside for the purpose by the Swiss National Insurance Company, Basle.

If German-speaking populations are, in general, quick to see the point of the new American painting, several reasons may be adduced. Most visitors, for instance, had been near enough to the point of complete physical catastrophe to have the mystique of the "fresh start" at their nerve ends. Expressionism has always been welcome, for its own sake, east of the Rhine. Many visitors, too, had lived through the long severance—1933-45—of German Europe from any real contact with the development of modern art; this, paradoxically, may have made it easier for them to identify themselves with the heedless energy of what Sam Hunter once called "a limited but intense wrecking enterprise directed against the 'good taste' and shallow eclecticism of provincial art culture." And it could also be said, without malice, that the Germans like a strong lead, and respond to it.

Will Grohmann, the veteran biographer of Kandinsky and Klee, spoke of the feelings, akin to terror, with which a European of his generation watched "these young Americans" (in itself a curious phrase to use of painters whose average age was fifty) "who stand beyond all questions of heritage and psychology, and almost beyond good and evil." The critic of the *Frankfurter Allgemeine Zeitung* was, on the whole, as enthusiastic as he was perceptive. "But," he felt bound to add, "not all these artists can fill their huge canvases with authentic intensity. The hoped-for vibration does not always materialize. Sometimes there are empty shells which remind us of the vacuous gesticulations of baroque painting (the Bolognese school, Luca Giordano, the 'studio of Rubens') and, even worse, of the 'history-pieces' of the nineteenth-century academicians."

In Milan and Madrid and Amsterdam and Brussels, reactions to the "New American Painting" show were cut more or less to pattern, with merely such local variants as might have been predicted—including a particular grossness in the anathemas of the Belgian press, where the paintings were said by one critic to "exceed by far the worst imaginable excesses, as regards indigence, imitative mediocrity, and poverty of intellect."

It was noticeable, however, that in Spain, which has developed for itself a group of younger modern painters unexcelled anywhere in Europe, the new American painting was seen in terms not of art politics, but of the general predicament of mankind as a whole. In *La Estafeta Literaria,* for instance, Joaquin de la Puente wrote: "Today we are at the beginning of a new battle against Nature. Man has penetrated a natural world unknown to former generations: that of an energy so great that, unless we keep it in control, it will be the end of us. The ancient terror of Nature's mysteries has given place to an invincible fear of what may follow the violation of those mysteries." Just as realism, in his view, belongs to the ages in which Man does not tremble before Nature, so the new American painting seemed to him to have been called forth in response to the disquiets of our day.

More important than any of these, in some respects, was the showing in Paris, where the "New American Painting" exhibition and the Jackson Pollock retrospective were put on simultaneously at the Musée d'Art Moderne. The notion of American predominance in modern art would be unwelcome in Paris at any time; today, at the very moment when the Fifth Republic is trying so hard to re-erect the concept of *la gloire,* it has a positively spectral quality. Paris takes its own pre-eminence so much for granted that very few French people realize how long it is since France nurtured a new painter of world consequence. (Even Dubuffet is a man of nearly sixty.) The French pavilion at the Venice Biennale has presented, for some years past, a spectacle of overconfidence as dismaying to the artists concerned as to the foreign visitor. In last year's "Fifty Years of Modern Art" at the Brussels Fair, only the French painters born before 1900 made a commanding impression, and great bitterness resulted among those who have on their hands, in Paris, both a perfected sales machine and a self-esteem such as even Rome in the seventeenth century would have envied.

It would be fair to say that the French authorities were not exactly eager to put on the American exhibitions, any more than the French critics were on fire to praise them. There was little enough, certainly, in the public prints that smacked of genuine enthusiasm. One veteran critic, M. Claude Roger-Marx, thought that such things should never have been shown in an official building at all. It was a delight to find, in the article by Professor André Chastel in *Le Monde,* the classic French virtues of lucidity, learning, and delicate analysis, with no admixture of mere trumpery matter. In

1952, when the Galerie de France showed a group of American paintings assembled by Sidney Janis, Chastel had considered that "the vital sources here are those of central European expressionism" and that "the results are apt to be all the more uncertain for the ardor with which they are produced." But in 1959 Chastel had come to acknowledge the purely native element in the new American painting: "the headlong, elemental movement, the exuberance of feeling, the naïveté of the New World." These are qualities which could result either in complete failure to communicate anything of significance or in a strikingly unified and harmonious ensemble. There was also the paradox of the denial of "the very idea of art," as a result of which the painter "hurls himself into experiments in which he will be forced to discover, in fear and trembling, the meaning of the very values he has denied."

"We are here concerned," Chastel went on, "with a form of painting which refuses to be 'sited,' or pinned down, or confined in any way. It will run into great difficulties when the time comes for it to grow old." And later, after setting against the native elements in this painting the effect of those Europeans who, from Hans Hofmann onwards, have lived in the United States for varying lengths of time, he suggested that American and European painters were engaged, whether wittingly or not, in a "difficult and tentative dialogue" which had for its theme the notion of the "object"

and the privileged autonomy of the painting treated as such.

In Moscow, where this summer's American art exhibition included instances of Pollock, De Kooning, and others, a preliminary salvo was fired, on June 10, in the course of a two-hour lecture by Alfred H. Barr of The Museum of Modern Art. His audience was, of course, hand-picked; but among the hundred-odd Soviet artists who heard him, saw the hundred and fifty color slides of American paintings which he threw onto the screen, and watched films of Calder and Pollock at work, one or two, at the very least, will have taken fire. The Soviet official who returned formal thanks to Mr. Barr is reported to have said that "many years ago the Russian artist Malevich painted a famous black square. Two generations have passed, but abstract painters are still at that same point." But "each generation," Mr. Barr replied, "must paint its own black square"; and I suspect that many in his audience agreed with him.

We in England are by no means of one voice in the matter of the new American painting: the extreme right still talks of "muck; lucrative muck" and the extreme left of "great talent made meaningless: one of the most dramatic examples of a society strangling its young." Even these reactions show, I think, that in an age when the image, as such, is everywhere debased, we can be grateful to the new American painters for proving that paint on canvas can still be one of the most exciting and controversial forms of human expression.

An American Dissent: *"We have been had"*

The European "discovery" of American abstract expressionism may be occurring at the very moment when, by ironic coincidence, this school of painting receives an overdue baptism of fire from the inner citadel of American art criticism. Taking over as art editor of The New York Times, *John Canaday aimed his opening gun at the dominant school of modern painting:*

There can be no objection to abstract expressionism as one manifestation of this complicated time of ours. The best abstract expressionists are as good as ever they were—a statement not meant to carry a concealed edge. But as for the freaks, the charlatans and the misled who surround this handful of serious and talented artists, let us admit at least that the nature of abstract expressionism allows exceptional tolerance for incompetence and deception. . . .

The question is why so many painters have adopted a form of art that should seem pointless except to the recondite, and why a large public is so humble in the face of an art that violates every one of its esthetic convictions. Bad painters we must always have, but how does it happen that we have them in such profusion in such a limited field, and why are we taking them so seriously? . . .

We suffer, actually, from a kind of mass guilt complex. Because Delacroix was spurned by the Academy until he was old and sick, because Courbet had to build his own exhibition hall in 1855 to get a showing for pictures that are now in the Louvre,

because Manet was laughed at, because Cézanne worked in obscurity, because Van Gogh sold only one picture during his lifetime, because Gauguin died in poverty . . . because of all this we have tried to atone to a current generation of pretenders to martyrdom. Somewhere at the basis of their thinking, and the thinking of several generations of college students who have taken the art appreciation course, is the premise that wild unintelligibility alone places a contemporary artist in line with great men who were misunderstood by their contemporaries.

Recognizing a Frankenstein's monster when they see it—and lately they can't miss it—some critics and teachers wail, "But what are we going to do? We can't go back to all those old Grant Woods again." Of course it is not a matter of going backward, but forward—somewhere. That we will go forward from abstract expressionism seems unlikely, since it is more and more evident that these artists have either reached the end of a blind alley or painted themselves into a corner. In either case, they are milling around in a very small area—which, come to think of it, may explain why they are increasingly under a compulsion to paint such very large canvases.

In the meanwhile, critics and educators have been hoist with their own petard, sold down the river. We have been had. In the most wonderful and terrible time of history, the abstract expressionists have responded with the narrowest and most lopsided art on record. Never before have painters found so little in so much.

Carol Reed directs "OUR MAN IN HAVANA"

CONTINUED FROM PAGE 31

thinking of their next picture and are willing to turn the current one over to the studio to cut. They're apt to say, 'I'm too close to the picture now.' That's nonsense. To make a good film you've got to sit down at the moviola day after day—all day—running the footage over and over, trying combinations.

"After you've been shooting awhile and are looking at your footage as you go, you begin to see the picture taking shape, establishing a rhythm of its own. Things begin to fall into place of themselves. That's when you begin to feel the picture's natural pace and you develop it. You can then work with the actors to mold and shape it. For instance, in a certain scene you may observe that a secondary character stands out, while your principal does not. So then you may decide to build that character up, while playing down your principal. This may give you something stronger, more compelling."

"What decided you upon making *Our Man in Havana* in black-and-white?" I asked.

"I've never seen a comedy in color, not a good one," said Reed. "You cannot seem to get it. Color is just not *real* enough yet. Perhaps it is for television, where your audience is sitting in a room with the lights on. But in a dark theater, confronted by that huge screen, I feel that it is just not convincing.

"Another thing. The color of Havana may seem exotic to us, coming from London or New York. But in a film made for the international market—as you must make films today, because of economics—the color of Havana will not seem so different from the color of the Mediterranean or Southeast Asia to the audiences of those countries."

I asked what qualities he looked for in actors. "Let me say this," he replied. "There are certain things actors do which you like them for; others have a way of doing things for which you cannot bear them. You know, Brando is a great actor. But today all the young men are trying to copy him, at least trying to acquire his force. Now the average leading man is afraid of being polite for fear of being thought effeminate. It's ridiculous. For me Cary Grant and Rex Harrison are the most brilliant players of light comedy today. Both are absolute masters of timing."

Thinking about the prestigious cast with which he was working and the considerable variation in their acting styles, and particularly in their speech, I mentioned this to Sir Carol. "Does it present any problems?"

"You know, the English language is not very elastic," he replied. "It makes for noble poetry, but in fact it is quite constrained; as a tongue it's narrow. Consider the words, 'I love you.' It's hard to speak them in such a way that they are not banal, awkward, or simply ridiculous in a film, particularly in a close-up. English simply doesn't have the fiery, emotional rhythms of a dramatic language such as Italian or French, or even German. Thus I think that variations in the speech patterns of players make for interest, especially when you are trying to convey the international flavor of a city like Havana.

"Likewise I feel that it is stimulating, especially for me, to see actors of different styles and habits working together in a film. A star like Alec Guinness is apt to stand out from the people around him by the subtle things he does. Now in this film, the character he plays is a plain man. It is important that he should not stand out. With people like Ives and Kovacs, even Maureen O'Hara, who are striking and positive types, he falls into place. It's better that way."

"You mentioned the effectiveness of black-and-white for comedy. Is this film a satire?" I asked.

"Not really," said Sir Carol. "Oh well, I suppose it is. But I am trying to bring out in it the more serious qualities which Graham Greene wrote into his story. Think about it for a minute. There are serious themes. After all, it examines loyalty and where one's true loyalty lies, to country or to one's loved ones when these come into conflict. I don't mean that it should be a message play. There should be nothing obvious, but underneath there are ideas of which some viewers will be aware."

"Do you believe that comedy—like other art forms—may be of a higher order when it proceeds on more than one level, when it is not being merely funny?"

"Oh, this must never be funny. It starts out quite seriously. Wormold-Guinness has been alone so long, left by his wife. A pretty serious fellow about his job, concerned with what the front office thinks. He's upset about having to handle this new Atomic Pile Cleaner. He's not at all sure it will sell. He hasn't had any fun for a long time. Then, with great reluctance, he gets into this spy business, but only in order to provide for the daughter he loves so much.

"The picture begins seriously. It is only after some success in practicing his delusion on the British Secret Service, and when the easy money begins to come in, that Wormold begins to relax. He thinks that it's going well. He is now a bit affluent, becomes a little expansive and his natural humor begins to emerge. It should do so naturally. It would be easy to make a funny picture, starting from the very idea of our man in Havana. But that wouldn't be enough."

"Reading the book and the script, one feels that it's satirical," I said, "that it laughs at bureaucratic institutions and functionaries slavishly carrying out commands. One sees very readily that it could be terribly comic with Alec Guinness in his familiar role as the little man in over his head, surrounded by desperate men. On the other hand, it's easy to see the film being a melodrama."

"Yes, the story changes," replied Reed. "It becomes melodrama, but only toward the end. I think we have time to develop our characters and to bring the audience along, finally giving them melodrama. And, of course, there are techniques for creating this change in mood. At the beginning I feel we should light our sets for comedy. That is, rather brightly and flatly, catching the beauty of the streets too. Then, as the picture moves toward melodrama, we will shoot with a wide angle, getting the effects of the walls closing in. We will use sharp hard lights in the night exteriors, making the streets slick and shiny, getting a brittle black-and-white feeling.

"Remember, Wormold makes a decision. He decides where his true loyalties lie and he rises to the occasion and acts. He isn't hurting his country, but he fights for those he loves."

"Even for Dr. Hasselbacher, who eventually betrays him?"

"Exactly! Wormold kills a man, but even then he is funny. One ought to feel he is not comically funny, but humanly. The role of his opponent, the 'other' agent, is going to be played by Paul Rogers. A fine actor, very strong. Again, his contrast to Guinness's restraint should count. The banquet scene, where he tries to poison Wormold, is crucial."

At this juncture, Sir Carol was called to the room telephone by the night clerk. He returned in a moment and excused himself. "I really must drop by to chat with Alec about some work he has been rehearsing." It was then 2 A.M.

Operations next day were at the Tropicana, one of this planet's most startling casino-nightclubs, a gaudy structure of concrete shells in the shape of a French cream roll, with lofty trees sprouting through the roof and catwalks for the chorus line extending out among the gardens of fern and bougainvillaea. It was in this exotic setting, rented for the purpose during daytime hours, that Reed proposed to stage a scene in which the principal characters are thrown together in a most unexpected way.

The occasion that brings Wormold and his daughter to the nightclub, accompanied by their old friend Dr. Hasselbacher, is Milly's seventeenth birthday. There is to be a birthday cake, artfully done to look like a snow-covered mountain with a skier fixed on it amid miniature firs, symbolizing Milly's future at school in Switzerland. All three are having a merry time, although Hasselbacher is somewhat reserved and Wormold slightly tipsy on champagne. A significant exchange takes place when Wormold declaims

"At seventeen years many their fortunes seek;
But at fourscore it is too late a week"

—and Milly proudly identifies it as a quotation from *As You Like It,* indicating that she has been stimulated to read Shakespeare since her father has been keeping a copy of Lamb's *Tales from Shakespeare* by his bed. Hasselbacher is immediately interested, but Wormold tries to pass over the matter. The audience will note Hasselbacher's sudden interest, for they have already learned that Lamb's *Tales* is the basis for the book code with which Wormold communicates with London. At this moment the suave but sinister Captain Segura intrudes himself at the table, taking over the party, barely noticing Wormold and thrusting his attentions upon Milly. Wormold is visibly contemplating braining Segura with a champagne bottle when his eye catches that of a handsome girl at the bar behind them. She senses what is passing through his mind and, pointing her siphon at Segura, directs a stream of water at his neck. He leaps to his feet and is astounded to find his assailant is a lady, who feigns innocence. There is a chilly exchange between them and the captain stalks off. Wormold introduces himself to the heroine and they dance, whereupon Wormold is staggered to learn that the girl is his new assistant, just arrived from London.

This scene, No. 46 in the script, is to play perhaps seven minutes. It is meant to be at once hilarious and scary as we first get the idea that Dr. Hasselbacher may be a friend to watch out for, then realize that this somewhat ungovernable lady spy will be a hazard as an ally who is marked by Captain Segura.

Sir Carol planned to shoot only the angles which showed the principals against the background of the crowd and floor show. He would shoot reverse angles showing them against the bar when they returned to the studios in England, where, he said, he would have far greater control over the lighting for important close-ups.

Filming Scene 46 involved careful planning and logistics. In order not to interrupt the flow of coin into the vault of the casino (business was meager during the tourist drought following the revolution) all the paraphernalia of the movie company had to be removed at the end of the day to make way for the guests. This meant erecting and dismounting scaffolds for the heavy arc lights, hauling in and out thousands of feet of cable and hundreds of props. Sir Carol's assistants had gathered several hundred of the prettiest girls in Havana with escorts, including the sugar daddies of which Cuba may have created the archetype. This herd had to be fed and given periodic refreshments. They had to be rehearsed in the matter of miming—dancing and lounging at the tables—during the "takes" so that the actors' voices would be audible.

When I arrived on the set this throng and the principals were assembled. The prop men were distributing the empty bottles to the tables and passing out cigars to the extras. Some assistant had maneuvered the most dazzling girls into the foreground—whence Gerry O'Hara, the first assistant director, moved them so that attention would not be diverted from the stars. Sir Carol was strolling about idly, examining the flora, and some of the more eye-catching fauna who were going through their paces. During the next two days, the chorus girls would go through their act fifty times, smiling and wiggling unflaggingly, although most of the time they would be out of the format or, at best, pinpoints in it.

Sir Carol was wearing a *guayabera,* the traditional Cuban shirt, open at the neck and worn outside the trousers. His reliance upon his assistants for all preliminaries and his consequent relaxation set him apart from the several hundred others present. When everything was set, the assistants rehearsed

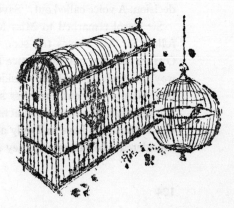

the extras as they danced and walked to and from the tables. Then Sir Carol took over. The first shots were long shots, to establish the wonders of the room and its inhabitants. This occupied the morning.

A man of the nicest manner, courteous to everyone, seldom giving a sign of impatience even under occasional conditions that might have taxed Saint Anthony, Reed was clearly a man preoccupied with his task. That afternoon he bent to it. Assembling his principals at a round table, he explained to them that the scene they were about to undertake was a key one in the film. Quietly he observed to Guinness that later on in the action Milly would think that he, Wormold, had picked up Beatrice, his new secretary, on the evening of the birthday party and that subtle grounds for this must be established. After Reed's briefing, they rehearsed the first movements of Scene 46. When it begins Milly is standing, playing with some spurs she has been given and looking over the crowd (which is going through its business under the scrutiny of two assistant directors); the birthday cake is carried in and Milly goes back to the table and sits down.

Sir Carol remarked that it would be simpler if the birthday cake were already on the table. All agreed. Sir Alec arranged the champagne bucket to his liking and they rehearsed the opening several more times. The cake, which had started to wilt under the hot lights, was removed by the property man. Sir Alec, looking cool in linen, was perspiring freely and had his jacket off, as did Burl Ives. The principals stepped away, stand-ins took their places for a final adjustment of lights and a checking of focus. The principals were recalled; the cake was popped out of a box; the hairdresser patted Sir Alec's head-covering; he and Burl Ives were sponged off by the make-up men; the glasses were repolished, ashtrays partially emptied; and Miss Morrow's gown was adjusted. Sir Alec directed the electrician to adjust his key light. Sir Carol said softly, "All right, let's make it."

As Milly turns around from watching the dancers and sits down Wormold, who has risen, says, "On this auspicious occasion. . . ." He looks where Miss O'Hara will be standing when they subsequently shoot the other angles in England and toasts her silently with his glass.

Sir Carol said gently, "Cut it," and a horn announced this decision. A voice called out, "Save the arcs."

Sir Carol remarked to Miss Morrow that she should not follow Sir Alec's eyes too soon when he looks where Miss O'Hara will be, but just notice him smiling, then look that way. He took Miss Morrow aside and had a few words with her. After a moment Guinness strolled over to him and remarked that perhaps he was acting too tipsy for a chap who was supposed to have had only a bit of champagne. The two considered whether or not they should assume he had been

drinking daiquiris, but decided against it. Then they ran through another rehearsal in which Guinness acted a shade less tipsy. He and Reed were both pleased. Another take was made. In all, seven takes were made of this action, which would constitute perhaps twenty seconds of the scene. After each Sir Carol and Sir Alec talked over the smallest details of what had just been filmed; then it would be played differently.

After each take, property men busied themselves reviving the pesky cake; Miss Morrow had the hem of her dress pressed on an adjacent table top; Mr. Ives was given a new cigar to light; Sir Alec slipped in and out of his coat and had his make-up touched up. It was a long afternoon and far from spent. When Sir Carol was finally satisfied and ordered the last two takes printed, a still-cameraman photographed the table with all its debris, so that it could be precisely duplicated to match this stage of the action, when they resumed filming in England.

To capture the rest of Scene 46 on film, eleven shots numbering 124 to 134 were made, each requiring from two to seven takes. In 125 Reed made a departure from the script. When Wormold spouts the quotation, instead of having Milly break in with the identification, Reed chose to have Dr. Hasselbacher remark, "Shakespeare, *As You Like It*"; then have Milly add, "It isn't in Lamb's *Tales*, I know." The effect is to hint much more clearly that Dr. Hasselbacher has been brushing up on *his* Shakespeare recently. One take was made, after which Sir Carol asked Burl Ives to "take your reaction down just a hair." He did it perfectly on the next try.

The following day was Sunday and the production supervisor, Ray Anzarut, decided to pay the high price of double-time salaries instead of sitting idle at a greater cost. The set was like a monstrous oven when the lights went on at 10:30 A.M. Activities were launched with Shot 128, the rude intrusion of Captain Segura.

Mr. Kovacs, who off the set was every instant the jolly joker of his television fame, showed himself on camera to be a professional who could perform in this league. A good deal of rehearsing and a number of takes went on while Sir Alec determined to his satisfaction and to Sir Carol's what Wormold's reaction to the police officer's rudeness should be.

At one point I observed Guinness had the director aside and was standing in front of him acting like the India Rubber Man in a freak show, sliding on and off his face a series of expressions signifying various degrees of bibulous annoyance. The display was a lexicon of eyebrow arching. In the subsequent days that I watched Guinness, I became aware that so great is the man's precision as an actor that he tints his performance as if he possessed a psychic eye-dropper and could add a drop of clownery or a drop of sadness, a drop of hesitancy or a drop of boldness as required. He and Sir Carol would converse and one or the other would say "down a shade," or "a hair more hesitant," and, presto! at the next take, his characterization of Wormold was just that hair different.

The high spot of the afternoon's toil came with the dousing of Captain Segura. During the lunch break I had looked on while Gerry O'Hara and his colleagues experimented with a battery of waterworks. Sir Carol had said sternly that he wanted a "good stream" to hit Mr. Kovacs. Bob Murrell, the property man, had fetched a soda siphon from Jamaica. It was loaded with a carbon dioxide cartridge and found wanting. After some testing, Gerry O'Hara fixed upon a garden hose, which he would bend to build up pressure, then release on cue.

This business was tried out several times on a stand-in. Then Mr. Kovacs manfully took his place. Four takes were made of Shot 131. In one the geyser caught Mr. Kovacs in the ear, in the others it soaked him generally. Between each take he had to take his uniform jacket off and put on a spare while the other was dried and pressed. He was patient, but director Reed was not enchanted with the accuracy of the attack. He stood there, hands behind his back, rhythmically clenching his teeth.

Sir Carol suggested to Mr. Kovacs how he thought Segura felt. Mr. Kovacs played the scene again, leaping up after his drenching to address Miss O'Hara venomously, but with chilling aplomb. He was a frightening Batista-type police chief. Sir Carol expressed satisfaction.

Mr. Kovacs went off to shed his dripping costume, and Sir Carol proceeded to photograph part of the first exchange between Wormold and Beatrice, which went off well and quickly.

After a short time Mr. Kovacs came back to bid good-bye to the principals still working: Sir Alec, Burl Ives, the Misses O'Hara and Morrow. He sat down off camera. Softly, Sir Carol ordered it to roll, and out of nowhere a huge stream of water smote the freshly dressed Mr. Kovacs, who leaped to his feet with a bellow. The camera recorded the genuine astonishment on the faces of the three seated at the table, Guinness, Ives, and Morrow, which was what Sir Carol wanted. "Very nice, Ernest," he said, "hope you don't mind; I needed that reaction, you know. You were first-rate." With everyone laughing, the Tropicana set was struck. Scene 46 had taken two days to shoot, had involved 350 people, and had cost $48,000 out of a total production budget of $2,000,000.

Sir Carol found some of his most vexatious work in the Shanghai Theatre. During the Batista reign the Shanghai Theatre had been an unsavory public spectacle, offering a dirty stage show and filthier movies. There was no more naked chorus in the world. In Graham Greene's novel and script, laid in the Batista period, the Shanghai is brought in when Wormold picks the name Teresa off its billboard to send back to London as one of the subagents he has hired. After Beatrice appears on the scene and they discover that real spies are operating against them, she dragoons Wormold into going to the Shanghai to warn Teresa. An uproarious scene follows, when they meet the stripper whom Wormold has pretended to hire for his fake spy ring.

Under the Castro clean-up the Shanghai had purified its show. Most of the old chorus had been jailed or banished from public appearances. To re-create the Shanghai atmosphere of the Batista era Sir Carol's agents had got back most of the old chorus, and although they were partially covered, they were a beat-up vision to behold. The "press gang" had also rounded up a crew of extras who looked like the real customers—and probably were. Being paid and given free cigars to boot, they let out whistles, cat-calls, and worse, when Pepe, an assistant director, urged them on. The action required Sir Alec and Maureen O'Hara to clamber into the front row, while the show roared on, and briefly to sit there talking, then force their way past the manager, through the stage door.

Everything got started. The razz-ma-tazz band started honking; the girls started stripping. But a government censor (who was happily acting as an extra in the audience) leaped up from time to time to order a girl's drawers yanked higher, or in one case lower, as his viewpoint was offended. How to get the effect of a rough show without showing it? Sir Carol had the answer. He would stand up among the undulating damsels with the camera beside him pointing at the audience. He would throw some intimate apparel out toward the grateful spectators so that the camera would catch them grabbing for the items. He did so. The audience threw them back so the action could be repeated. This brought the censor up, howling that the show looked truly immoral. He stopped the filming. He demanded that the whole day's negative be turned over to him. Sir Carol, with thousands of dollars invested in it, held firm. Hours dragged by until Sir Carol signed some deposition concerning what he would or wouldn't do with the shot. Said Gerry O'Hara, "We could have set the whole thing up in the studio, and a lot naughtier too." Only a few days before, the censor had stopped production until the real shoeshine boy in a bar scene could get clean trousers on. Shoeshine boys in Havana are not to be shown with dirty knees.

That evening, with the temperature hung up like the toasted marshmallow moon in the Cuban sky, Gerry O'Hara and I sat in a deserted French bar opposite the hotel. I asked him the secret of Reed's genius as a motion-picture director.

"Absolute immersion in his story," O'Hara said. "It is partly why he listens to so much bull. A lot of directors would say 'toddle off, old boy.' Carol hears everybody out. All he is thinking about is 'are they hurting my picture?' You can always tell a bad director if he worries about the background or whether the lights are ready; or if he comes on the set stalling for time and saying, 'let's move the furniture,' so that he can work out his scene. Carol has worked out that scene and all the others months before shooting. More important than that, he cares deeply about the story and focuses on what is going on between the people in a scene.

"The man's concentration is phenomenal. He has a wonderful way of measuring the significance of a situation and what he wants it to add up to. And he works for subtle effects. Have you noticed the young Cuban boy and girl who are in the background of so many shots?"

"Yes, I have," I said, "and the older man, who often appears when they don't."

"Right," said Gerry. "To begin with you will see the girl and the young man in the title background. She is leaning out of a balcony; the young man is leaning against the wall. Then she goes in and comes down in the street and goes off with the young man. But she leaves her scarf behind and a little while later her husband finds it and sets out after her. You see the three over and over throughout the film; never obtrusively, for Carol has always shot them so that they could be cut out if he chooses. You know, they walk in after the significant action ends."

"What's it all about?" I asked.

"Carol has thought out all the details of their lives, though none of this is in the script. The boy is from the country. It is his first day in the city. The girl is married to the older man and restless. They are attracted to one another and she goes off with him. The husband sets out to find her. They are woven all through the film, but most people will never notice them. No one will know these particulars, but Carol could tell you the whole story of their lives after the period of our film.

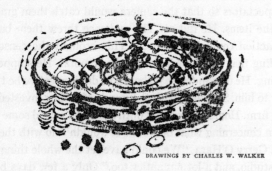

DRAWINGS BY CHARLES W. WALKER

Later that night, talking with Barbara Hopkins, the sound-recordist, I picked up another clue about Reed's passion.

"Do you remember the theme music from *The Third Man?*" she asked.

Like the terrifying camera angles in his *Fallen Idol,* it was a Carol Reed touch one didn't forget.

"Having discovered Anton Karas in Vienna, he had him virtually living in his home while they finished the picture," said Barbara. "One night Karas had been under Carol's kitchen table playing the zither. Well, a bit later, when they were recording the music at the studio, Carol didn't like what he heard and told Karas and the sound-lads that he wanted it to sound like what he had heard at home that night. He asked Karas to play under a table. Still not right. So Carol had his kitchen table brought to the studio. That's a man who knows what he wants."

That evening I sat down again over a daiquiri with an exhausted Carol Reed. "You said recently that you hoped there

was not a Carol Reed style," I ventured, "and yet I cannot help seeing certain characteristics in your films. You've talked about their pace. They also frequently seem to be constructed with the tension and suspense familiar and appropriate to melodrama. Doesn't this suggest that a certain type of story engages you more than another?"

"What interests me," he replied, "is a situation in which a group of people are confronted by a problem, rather than just the situation of two people trying to get together. I suppose my background has something to do with my seeing appealing values in melodrama. As a young man in the theater I became an assistant to Edgar Wallace, who wrote and produced so many melodramas. I suppose I got used to them, saw their effectiveness."

"I must say that I cannot think of many of your films in which the man and woman get together."

"They don't always in life," said Sir Carol. "I don't think you need a happy ending."

I mentioned his recent picture, *The Key,* and the fact that New York City saw it with an unhappy ending—Bill Holden missing Sophia Loren—while the rest of the country saw him catching up with her.

"Yes, that was absolutely silly," said Sir Carol. "I believe it was a mistake. I did not produce that film as I usually do. I took on a script that had been quite developed. When we were nearly done I was persuaded that too much rode on the success of this picture to be risked on a downbeat ending. The picture was much stronger with the two missing one another. I don't like to tie things up too neatly. Life isn't like that. You know, all that happens in life is through loneliness. It hurls people into trouble and it leads people into happiness.

"Now take Wormold and Beatrice at the end of this story. I don't know whether they are going off together forever. They may make love or not. I think after awhile they may get married. But if they do, it will be eventually, casually, almost by accident."

And then for fifteen minutes, Reed speculated in great detail about the two characters' lives beyond the termination of Graham Greene's novel. I hesitated to interrupt but did.

"What purpose do the young boy and girl and the older husband serve—those three who appear on the fringes of so many scenes?"

He looked surprised. "They are only there for those who find them. The picture should not be any less successful for those who do not. They are just there."

"But what do they mean? Do they suggest that lovers may be fated for one another, as a parallel to the story of Wormold and Beatrice? Or do they somehow say that one can never escape the obligations of love, or of matrimony? Do they serve to make some commentary?"

Sir Carol looked thoughtful and faraway. "If I told you what I thought they may mean, you would think I was pompous or a fool. They are there now, and I think they will be when the picture is finished. I'm not sure. They are just there."

Olivetti: A Man and A Style

CONTINUED FROM PAGE 51

pristine white walls, occasionally enlivened with blown-up photostats of Picasso etchings and lithographs. The effect suggests that Rome and national affairs will always be an outpost for Olivetti, and that his true home is elsewhere.

Yet his new public life is foremost in his thoughts. "Until 1934," he told me, "I busied myself with business affairs, learning and doing as much as I could. But after 1934 I realized how important the outside world was, how one could not proceed without accepting it and using it and finally changing it."

"And finally changing it": remarkable words to hear from a European industrialist. Yet he has obviously meant them. During a year's exile in Switzerland, at the height of Italy's wartime nazification, he developed an elaborate theory of Italian reconstruction along regional lines: "I was sure that the existing political philosophies were inadequate. Liberalism, socialism, Christian socialism—they were so abstract. I set out to conceive a new political theory and I worked eight years in developing that of the community. It was a new conception of functionalism in politics. Among the thinkers who influenced me were Maritain, Berdyaev, Mounier, and Simone Weil. It is shaped by Italian conditions with their strong tradition of region and community. But now local governments are poor and are attacked by the central government. I would like to do something about this."

Olivetti, who is fond of quoting himself, then picked up one of his articles and read: "The fundamental idea of this new society is to create a common moral and material interest among the people who live their social and economic lives in a geographical area neither too large nor too small, that by nature and history has been given its own identity."

Returning home from Switzerland, Olivetti founded the Community Movement (*Movimento Communità*) around his idea, and soon found himself involved in local, and then national politics. He also threw himself into publishing with his own book house, *Edizioni di Communità,* and the magazines *Communità, Sele Arte, Zodiac,* and others, all designed to propound his views on society and art and to circulate the works of anyone in whom he recognized a kindred spirit. His biggest publishing venture, the *Edizioni* (which it "took a crazy courage to begin," one of his associates remarks) has turned out Italian editions of authors ranging from Sartre to Silone, Koestler to Kierkegaard, Walter Lippmann to Le Corbusier, Gide to John Kenneth Galbraith. The choice of books is largely Olivetti's own. His magazines and pamphlets—often including portions of works of his own such as *The Political Order of the Community, Society, State and Community,* and *Community Ideals*—have inveighed against the shortcomings and corruption of political parties as Olivetti sees them. They echo his theorem that "Our hope lies in a life in which the goal of human endeavor

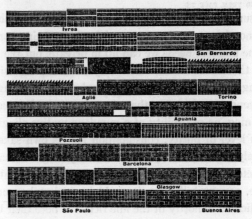

Part of advertisement shows 10 Olivetti plants.

is not money or power, but the good of the community—a community whose best sons may achieve their best aspirations, where a real civilization may flourish. And each man shall know that he is a member of a community greater than himself."

To some, this has smacked of an attempt to revive a corporate state; to others, of idealism mixed with well-meaning windiness and obscurantism. Two years ago, on trying to give his ideas the substance of political action, Olivetti was roundly rebuffed at the polls when all the nominees of his new *Communità* party save himself were rejected. Commenting on this fiasco, one ironical Roman remarked: "Lots of people in Italy deplore mass parties. But the only thing they can do is form another one."

But despite this political failure, Olivetti is not discouraged. "Around Ivrea," he remarked to me amid his isolation as a political deputy in Rome, "we have attempted to create a better civilization with deeper spiritual values and social peace. . . . You ask me what my ideal man would be? I believe that in Italy there are men who combine intelligence and feeling. This is what I want. These days such men are not powerful enough. We must found a state in which they can flourish. Our ruling class is mediocre. We must find a way to put the best men at the top. You see, I am an aristocrat in politics."

It may not be the function of a businessman in our time to propound, much less found, a state. An industrial lord plunging into politics today may find himself far beyond his depth. But the idea of aristocracy and responsibility mixed with daring does remain welcome, particularly in the arts and in the area of social reform. It is in these fields that *Il Ingegnere* Adriano Olivetti, whatever his other excursions, has shown himself past master.

Kermit Lansner is a senior editor of Newsweek, *and has written on art and literary subjects for various reviews.*

The Wreck of the Status System

CONTINUED FROM PAGE 25

Consumption, as Thorstein Veblen made sure that we would not forget, achieves its social role by being conspicuous. The minimal needs we can fill in private, but the spending of the excess fulfills itself only in being excessive—in breaking the bonds of practicality and sense, in voyaging so far beyond into frivolity that there is no turning back, no questioning, no possibility of a mundane motive clinging on. At this level of purity, consumption for its own sake is an extremely arduous affair; and in the early stages of mass culture, before the Keynesian economy began to operate full-throttle, responsibility for it could be undertaken only by the dedicated minority of the idle rich. We bore their burden of leisure and boredom vicariously, sparing ourselves the discovery of how onerous these interlocked gifts can be, and for this relief we granted them the aureole of our attentive curiosity, the iron crown of glamour which weighs down upon its bearers more heavily than the most painful privilege of kings and emperors.

But now idleness and wealth have been scattered with a generous hand, and everyone is condemned to be to some degree a consumer. The heady atmosphere of abundance even creates new and unheard-of ostentations, like the luxury of refusing to consume at all: of being "beat," of designing buildings without decoration, or of going on diets. "The difference between your country and mine," a Soviet Russian official said to me several months ago, "is that in Moscow now the signs in the stores say *high-calorie* bread."

No one is more victimized in this rat race than the well-to-do. Pity the poor rich—not the rich-rich (they always manage to get by) but the poor-rich, the people who live on large but taxable salaries, who imagine they have earned their way up in the world, who have accumulated expectations at a faster rate than even the really rich could realize them, and who are now struggling along on incomes they once thought of as permanent titles to privilege. I remember a number of years ago when an article called "Going Broke on $10,000 a Year" appeared in *Harper's,* and I was filled with scorn for the unhappy man who wrote it, thinking he had dug that bearpit for himself. Now it turns out that he was merely a forerunner. There are families that can scarcely make it on $50,000 a year, and none of their expenses—house, cars, servants, schooling, clubs, and charities—would have been considered out-of-the-ordinary for their status-level when its manner of life was being formed.

Here again we are prisoners of the past. Not everyone suffers as the rich do, nor so comfortably, but we are all involved in the gap between demand and satisfaction which is supposed to keep us busily at work, and to give our society its "dynamic" motive power. What is the incentive, if the goal is seen to be so dubious? I live in New York City, where the poor-rich are indeed persecuted, and compelled to live in superslums like the new apartment houses on Sutton Place, where they get nothing but low ceilings, thin walls, and a sliver of river view to console them for high rents, the surveillance of doormen, and the company of their kind. The rest of us are in a similar boat. It is said that we are all now members of the middle class, as though this were not a mixed blessing and did not mean, as it used to mean, "bourgeois" —with all its connotations of stiff collars, dark suits, and other ritual observances of the respectable. The requirement is the same, even if it results in living in a ranch house and owning a Pontiac.

Escape from consumption has been the goal of this generation's pioneers. The first to be saddled with leisure in vast quantity, they have valiantly struggled to assimilate it. According to the viewers-with-alarm, they were going to become passive and moronic—television was the villain normally cited here—and yet, while there is a limit to the claims that can be made for quality, the predictions of universal passivity have notably failed to materialize. Instead of occupying time, people have chosen to occupy themselves. They have deserted the spectator sports in droves. They have learned to do-it-yourself, to do dozens of the menial, handicraft functions that become—in a full-employment society— so expensive, and to find in them an unexpected outlet for what Veblen called the "instinct of workmanship." And some have even turned to the arts. One conference, summoned to deplore the low state of our commercial culture, was astonished by a bank vice-president who informed it that he was a member of a chamber-music group made up entirely of businessmen. He added that it was called the *Déjà-Vu* Quartet, which meant that while playing a piece they sometimes had the feeling of having heard it somewhere before.

We are anxious now about status because it is problematical, which is another way of saying that the system no longer works. We are no longer bound by birth or bankroll to a fixed place in it, and there is the opportunity—though no requirement—for the individual to escape. In this disorderly turmoil it is difficult to discover who one is, but it is uniquely possible now to be free from the social self, that person other people think we are, and to be free also from envy—that most vicious of the sins inherent in a stratified society. Freedom is not necessarily a pleasure. Abundance may appear to be the palliative of our ills, but it is not. It calls in question the most fundamental principles; our own purpose, that of our people. There has never been anything like it before, and we are on our own.

Eric Larrabee, Executive Editor of AMERICAN HERITAGE, *was editor of* American Panorama, *a survey of books about America prepared for the Carnegie Corporation, and of an anthology (with Rolf Meyerson) called* Mass Leisure.

THE SILENT TRAVELLER DRAWS THE WEST

A few winters ago a Chinese painter and writer named Chiang Yee slipped into Boston as silently as the snow. He had come to observe the city, and had chosen its least ingratiating season because, as he said, "I like to begin to know a place in winter." How well he came to know Boston could be judged this fall with the publication of *The Silent Traveller in Boston* (Norton). This is his tenth travel book, and like its predecessors it is a blend of odd perceptions, swift little drawings in Chinese ink, and such effortless evocations of a city's mood as the water color above of the Park Street Church with a swirl of pigeons at its feet. Some twenty-five years ago, Mr. Chiang was the governor of the Kiukiang District in China. This job enmeshed him in "five years of incessant talking"—something quite unsuited to his temperament—so he gave it up and left China. He took with him only his Chinese pen name, Ya-Hsin-Che, which can be translated literally as "Dumb Walking Man" but more elegantly as "The Silent Traveller." And this has given him his real vocation ever since he arrived in England in 1933: travelling about, talking little, hearing much, seeing the West with Chinese eyes, painting it with Chinese ink and colors, and reflecting on it with Confucian good sense.

In this portfolio HORIZON presents a sampling of the Silent Traveller's observations—in text, drawing, and water color—on Boston, New York, Oxford, Edinburgh, and Paris.

Louisburg Square

BOSTON

One warm night I lay awake in bed until at last I got up and went out for a stroll as I used to do in my homeland on summer nights years ago. . . . Here and there in the little garden of the Square I detected tiny lights winking and sparkling. They were glow-worms. At the same time my ears were filled with a soft music as intoxicating as that of familiar tunes I had heard in faraway Kiukiang. It was the chirp of crickets. . . . A summer night in Louisburg Square had brought back to me my childhood in my old home garden, laughing, chasing, quarrelling with girl and boy cousins while we tried to catch glow-worms or to play the cricket-fight game.

The Silent Traveller in Boston

Concord Bridge

CONCORD

"Concord is as pleasant and peaceful as ever before."
Indeed it is so, but it must have been through some
changes. For instance, the bridge that arches over the
Concord River today is not the one which used to be a
public thoroughfare in Paul Revere's days. Perhaps just
because it is not a public thoroughfare now, the river there
seems to be more peaceful than elsewhere. The monument
of the Minuteman hidden behind trees is not easy to see,
and is an unassuming one compared to the monuments of
war heroes on the European Continent. I have never seen
a place of great historic importance so in harmony with
its name.

The Silent Traveller in Boston

Fort Tryon Park

NEW YORK

When I turned along a footpath and stopped near a big tree I found myself in a totally different world—a silvery dream world. . . . The moonlight illuminated the tree leaves, the little rocks and even the tiniest petals of some wild flowers. Their colors were not emphasized as they would have been by sunlight, but were toned down as if each had been newly washed. Their freshness exhaled an atmosphere of tranquillity and soothed my mind. I felt disinclined to move, for the stillness of the shadows of trees and rocks seemed to influence me to keep still as well. Shadows in the daytime have beauty but no secrecy.

The Silent Traveller in New York

Radcliffe Square

OXFORD

In the soft late spring air a haze of peaceful antiquity seemed to permeate the very stones of the buildings. The round dominating dome of the Camera in the center; the St. Mary's spire; the dull yellow wall of Brasenose . . . all seemed to be taking part in a solemn atmospheric ceremonial service. Two professors in long black gowns and mortarboards came out of Brasenose College, and added, as it were, a touch of *human* antiquity to the scene. Yet there was a tinge of present-day atmosphere too . . . a few girl students in brightly colored jumpers and long trousers . . . and two W.A.A.F.S. who were examining the Camera.

The Silent Traveller in Oxford

133

Lady Stair's House

EDINBURGH

Having been brought up in Confucian respect for my elders I was touched by the kindness of this old man who was so anxious to show me the old part of the city, and I followed him closely. First we went to Riddle's Court . . . then we visited a few more closes, including Lady Stair's Close, where I was persuaded to walk a little way up the turnpike stairs. . . . What interested me most about him was that during all our time together he had been smoking the butt of a cigar fixed on to a penknife. . . . This is another characteristic in common between the Scots and the Chinese, for we too understand the principle of thrift.

The Silent Traveller in Edinburgh

134

Place de Furstemberg

PARIS

The quietness of the street and the clarity of the night scene contrasted strangely with what we had just left. As if by magic, I found myself leading Bastien to a nearby square to see how it looked by night. It was the Place de Furstemberg, in the corner of which was Delacroix's studio. This is one of the oldest spots in Paris, a beautiful square of which I was very fond. The street-lamps with their five milk-white balls were lit up. The shadows of the few bare trees were cast by the moon-light on the faded pinkish walls of the houses on the left, one of which was Delacroix's studio. Peace reigned as it must have reigned for decades.

The Silent Traveller in Paris

Jamaica Pond

BOSTON

Facing us came a troop of a countless quacking army from Duckland, a small island in the center of the pond with two little picturesque willows for decoration. . . . I let the boat drift for a moment and was astonished at the continuous line of ducks plunging down into the water from the little island to join the others in a semicircle as if under a strict order. . . . The ducks were floating on thin sheets of golden silk. . . . The warm colors of yellow, pink, and red breathed warmth all over us. Of all Boston experiences, rowing on Jamaica Pond in the beautiful autumn is one of my most memorable.

The Silent Traveller in Boston